The Ex-Offender's
Re-Entry Success Guide

Selected Books by Author

The Ex-Offender's Re-Entry Success Guide

Smart Choices for Making it on the Outside

Fourth Edition

Ronald L. Krannich, Ph.D.

IMPACT PUBLICATIONS
Manassas, VA

EDITION: Fourth

ISBNs: 978-1-57023-413-2 (paperback); 978-1-57023-415-6 (eBook)

PUBLISHER: For information on Impact Publications, visit www.impactpublications.com.

PUBLICITY/RIGHTS: For information on publicity, author interviews, and subsidiary rights, contact the Media Relations Department: Tel. 703-361-7300, Fax 703-335-9486, or email: query2@impactpublications.com.

SALES/DISTRIBUTION: All special sales and distribution inquiries should be directed to the publisher: Sales Department, IMPACT PUBLICATIONS, 7820 Sudley Road, Suite 100, Manassas, VA 20109, Tel. 703-361-7300, Fax 703-335-9486, or email: query2@impactpublications.com. All bookstores sales are handled through Impact's trade distributor: National Book Network, 15200 NBN Way, Blue Ridge Summit, PA 17214, Tel. 1-800-462-6420.

QUANTITY DISCOUNTS: We offer quantity discounts on bulk purchases. Please review our discount schedule for this book at www.impactpublications.com or contact the Special Sales Department, Tel. 703-361-7300.

THE AUTHOR: Ronald L. Krannich, Ph.D., is one of today's leading career and travel writers who has authored more than 100 books, including several self-help guides for ex-offenders: *The Ex-Offender's New Job Finding and Survival Guide, The Ex-Offender's Re-Entry Assistance Directory, Best Resumes and Letters for Ex-Offenders, The Ex-Offender's Job Interview Guide, Best Jobs for Ex-Offenders, The Ex-Offender's Re-Entry Success Guide, The Ex-Offender's Quick Job Hunting Guide, The Ex-Offender's 30/30 Job Solution, 99 Days to Re-Entry Success Journal, The Re-Entry Employment and Life Skills Pocket Guide, The Re-Entry Start-Up Pocket Guide, The Anger Management Pocket Guide, The Re-Entry Personal Finance Pocket Guide,* and *Re-Imagining Life on the Outside Pocket Guide.* A former Peace Corps Volunteer, Fulbright Scholar, and university professor, Ron specializes in producing and distributing books, DVDs, training programs, and related materials on employment, career transition, addiction, anger management, criminal justice, life skills, and travel.

INSTRUCTOR'S GUIDE: Free downloadable Instructor's Guide for group training available at www.impactpublications.com (click the hyperlink at the end of product #9947).

Contents

STEP 1

STEP 2

STEP 3

STEP 4

STEP 5

STEP 6

STEP 7

You CAN make it . . .
one smart step at a time!

1

What's Your Re-Entry I.Q.?

"What appears to be the end may really be a new beginning. The future belongs to those who create it one smart step at a time."

SO, YOU'VE MADE MISTAKES, experienced bad luck, suffered pain and injustices, and done time in a stinking cage where you learned the value of freedom. If you're like many other ex-offenders, incarceration has been a chilling and costly experience for both you and your family. You probably experienced some combination of fear, distrust, fragile hope, boredom, grief, and depression. Flushed and forgotten like human trash, this lockdown experience is something you want to forget as a low point in your life. Nothing good comes from it other than learning some important life lessons, such as never ever again end up in another cage. It's time to look up and savor the full sunshine of freedom and finally live the life you were meant to live!

Above all else, you need to **create a new mindset** that will help you **transform your life**. Start with contemplating some of the wise yet simple advice dispensed by noted writer H. Jackson Brown, Jr. (see pages 19-20). That's what this book is all about – changing your mindset for charting a new course that involves picking up the pieces and leaving this experience behind you. Yes, you're out for good! When you finally put on your street clothes and walk into the sunshine with your measly gate money, don't look back. Your future lies ahead. It requires making important decisions about who you really want to become – **the new you. Your future is now in your hands!**

Making Smart Choices

You've made **choices** that got you where you are today. And you've been held **responsible** for those choices. So, think about your most recent decisions and plans for getting your life back on track. What does your future look like in the weeks and months ahead? What do you plan to do with the rest of your life? No promises, no bull, no jiving, no games, no lies, no conning others or yourself – just good solid choices that are likely to produce results for re-entry success. Call this **making smart choices**.

If you're coming up empty or uncertain about what choices work best for ex-offenders, read on and complete the many exercises in the pages that follow. This workbook is all about making wise decisions and taking responsibility for your future. It's about

changing the behavior that was the source of your so-called misfortunes with the criminal justice system. It's a book for self-directed "people of light" rather than "people of heat" (see below) who want to stay out for good. No one can do this better than **you**!

You're not the only one making choices affecting your future. Other people will be judging you – your skills, character, motivation, self-discipline, personality, attitude, and mental health – and deciding whether or not to trust you. So what's next? Why should someone hire you? Who wants to rent you an apartment, live with you, extend you credit, become your friend, or give you a helping hand? Will they be making smart choices by associating with you? Why should they hang around an ex-offender who thinks he has done his time and thus everything should be fine?

What **new choices** have you made that could make a difference in your future? Have you changed your **mindset**? Do you have a **life plan**? What about a basic yet realistic **re-entry plan** from Day One to Day 90, or even to Day 180? Do you have a compelling and convincing **story** about how you've changed your life since lockdown? Can you provide good **evidence** – proof of rehabilitation – that you've changed your life for the better?

Are you going to make it on the outside or soon stumble back into the criminal justice system as another disappointing recidivism statistic? Will you change your life or demonstrate that you're not prepared to handle the Free World? Will "freedom" be just another word to repeat the same old mistakes that will probably bring you back to where you've wasted time, as well as your mind, sitting in a cage angry and blaming others for your sorry fate?

By the way, how have you spent your time since lockup? Exercising? Playing cards? Socializing with questionable characters? Feeling sorry for yourself? Conning others? Working with a mentor? What have you learned that will help you make it on the outside? What, for example, mind-enriching things have you read and learned during the past 12 months? What classes have you attended? What new skills have you acquired? Think about your values, goals, motivations, self-discipline, drive, character, self-esteem, and trustworthiness – how do they differ today from two years ago? In other words, what have you been doing with your mind to shape your future in a positive direction? Or are you one of those bored, idle, and angry coulda, woulda, shoulda types who has wasted time by simply doing time and tending to your body rather than to your mind. Do you spend most of your time exercising your muscles, talking trash, fantasizing, and making empty promises about doing better the next time out rather than taking specific actions to rewire your mind for re-entry success?

People of Light, People of Heat

It's an old story – most people make life-changing decisions when they either see the light or feel the heat. Some ex-offenders see the light early on in the incarceration process – through education, spiritual transformation, a mentor experience, and/or introspection. Perhaps they followed Ned Rollo's seasoned advice on how to best survive the correctional experience (*A Map Through the Maze*) by tending to their mind. Many

people of light experience an important **Aha! moment** when they decide it's time to make some significant changes in their life. Unlike unenlightened **people of heat**, people of light are sick and tired of life on the inside and accordingly take action. Better still, they see opportunities in the face of adversities. By changing their mindset, people of light see and follow a new path for re-entry success.

> *People of light discover a purpose in life that helps direct their future.*

Most important of all, people of light discover a **purpose** in life (see Chapters 5 and 10) that helps direct their future choices. That purpose results in developing productive attitudes, self-motivation, self-discipline, and new relationships. Laser-like, they focus on what's really important to living a meaningful life. While they are in a short-term situation, they plan for the long term. Seeing the light means they will never again need to take the heat!

But if you've not had **your Aha! moment**, you'll most likely remain in the dark and continue taking the heat rather than making changes that can lead to a satisfying and rewarding life. It's your choice – light or heat. If you don't see the light, expect to take more heat in the years ahead. By the way, people of light live much longer than people of heat who prematurely succumb to the life-shortening realities of the street and other forms of self-destructive behavior.

However secure, predictable, and comfortable, jail or prison is no place to live a life. After all, life is short and then you shorten it further by going to jail or prison. You need to get a real life, indeed a wonderful life, by becoming a person of light.

Dysfunctional Freedom, Broken Lives

Let's face it, at times we all make bad decisions and become losers. Unfortunately, some people have a propensity to repeatedly make unfortunate decisions that constantly mess up their lives. Indeed, they live broken and seemingly hopeless lives. If you have a long rap sheet, you need help with re-engineering your life. Such people are literally their own worst enemies. Self-centered, feeling victimized and angry, and lacking goals, self-motivation, and self-esteem, they seldom take responsibility for their actions. Working through denial, they lie or blame others, including "the system" that did everything bad to them. Unwilling to challenge their mindsets and change their lives, many of these people seem lost beyond repair. Even God Almighty and his prison helpers who harvest souls can't do much for such **institutionalized losers** except give them hope in the form of spiritual guidance. These are our people of heat who live dysfunctional lives alongside similarly dysfunctional people who share the same troubling mindsets. Unwilling to change, they decide to stay in the same old mental box as well as return again and again to similar steel and concrete cages.

But there is another way. As revealed throughout this book, "freedom" should be another word for **staying out for good**! You do this by developing a **new mindset** that emphasizes the importance of learning, self-transformation, self-motivation, self-discipline, personal responsibility, and smart decision-making. You are open to new ideas, different ways of thinking, and new approaches to reality.

Whether you recognize it or not, for better or for worse, you are a **work in progress**! It's time to help yourself in order to understand and experience the true meaning of freedom.

Making It on the Outside

For a variety of reasons, be it intelligence, character, psychological problems, disabilities, or lack of common sense, many people have a **pattern of misfortune** – screwing up and getting into social, financial, or legal trouble. Exhibiting a mindset of negative and delusional thinking, they make a **habit of failure** and get stamped **loser** on their forehead. Some get stuck in a seemingly endless criminal justice revolving door – in and out, out and in, and in and out. They temporarily clean up their act in prison or jail and then return to Freedom Street where they soon start the whole process over again of becoming a loser. Poster children for what's wrong with today's criminal justice system, and examples of personal failures, these ex-offenders also demonstrate that they lack sufficient intelligence, motivation, and character to become productive members of society. From a security perspective, such losers definitely need to be separated from society – caged, gated, and monitored until they reach that all important release date. Parole, probation, and halfway houses become tripwires for those who make poor choices that land them back in lockup.

Fortunately, some of these people bounce back by changing their mindset. They recognize their problems, take responsibility, and transform their lives by making smart decisions. Others never get it. They just repeat the same old patterns that have similar negative consequences. They epitomize the definition of **insanity** – repeat the same behaviors with the expectation of achieving different results or outcomes. Unless you are self-destructive, this is not the well-traveled road you want to take.

Been There, But Not Done It Yet

You'll soon be leaving prison and returning to the **Free World**. You've been dreaming of this day and what your life might become in the months and years ahead. Perhaps you've

> *If life is short, then doing time is a sure way of further shortening your life!*

been through the five stages of grief and discovered the transforming power of 12-step programs. You've dealt with boredom, anger, depression, addiction, self-esteem, attitude, motivation, responsibility, forgiveness, trustworthiness, and communication issues. Maybe you became religious, learned meditation, acquired a GED certificate and/or college credits, developed new work-related skills, and have a compelling story about your rehabilitation – experiences that give you a new purpose in life and make you more marketable in today's highly competitive job market.

But there's still lots of work to be done if you want to make it in the Free World . . . for good. That's what this book is all about – helping you develop that **extra edge** to make it on the outside. Never again should you lose one of life's most precious resources – **time**. As you know all too well, doing time means losing time as well as your mind. If life is short, then doing time is a sure way of further shortening your life!

Now It's Show Time

But now it's show time, a time to show what you've learned and what you're really made of. In fact, you face something you may not be prepared to deal with – a process called **re-entry** – moving from one **environment** (incarceration) to another (family, community, street). It's not an easy process. Indeed, it's often scary for those who have been off the street for a long time. The reality will vary for different individuals with different criminal and social backgrounds.

For example, you may be one of the lucky ones who was convicted of a nonviolent drug or petty theft offense, took advantage of correctional educational programs, and already have a job lined up as well as a very supportive family that will assist you with the daily necessities of life (housing, food, transportation, health care, pocket money). While you still have important re-entry issues, these are minor compared to the many re-entry problems facing other inmates you met on the inside. You're a person of light who makes relatively smart decisions and thus has a high probability of making it on the outside.

On the other hand, you may have been convicted of a violent crime or a sex offense, been diagnosed with psychological problems, behave impulsively, exhibit frightening body art, lack basic workplace skills, and now you're on your own and indigent. You think you're smart. In fact, you'll soon find out how smart you are back on the street. You literally have nothing to start your new life on the outside, and no one wants to help risky people with your type of criminal, psychological, and employment background. You may find a job, but you probably won't keep it long. You'll find many temptations to repeat old habits that will again land you in trouble and back into a cage. However difficult to achieve, you could use a complete makeover – a new you, from head to toe. Indeed, you'll need all the assistance you can find – a lifeline that will help you through some difficult times that lie ahead. Unfortunately, you have a high probability of not making it on the outside. If you want to be successful, you'll have to work much harder at this re-entry process than other ex-offenders. You need to experience a huge "Aha! moment" to see the light and then transform your life!.

Life Can Be Tough

Spending time in prison or jail is not how most people plan their lives. But it's not the end of the world – nearly everyone (95 percent) eventually gets out and transitions to a new life. Even under the best of circumstances, life can be tough. When you get out, perhaps you'll pick up where you left off, make up for lost time, and do many things you've been thinking of doing. Maybe you've changed your life, discovered a purpose, have goals, taken responsibility, and already lined up a job. Or maybe you're uncertain about your future and angry about your lost time. Whatever your situation, freedom will have different meanings as you move ahead with your life.

But wait a minute. Freedom can be a double-edged sword for ex-offenders. While leaving prison or jail with $200 of gate money and a few personal belongings may be physically liberating, the **psychological challenges** that lie ahead can be difficult even under the best of circumstances. Indeed, ex-offenders face numerous challenges when re-entering the Free World. As many of them readily admit, re-entering society can be as scary as going to jail or prison in the first place! Unfortunately, scared people often make bad decisions. Consider these five realities as you prepare for re-entry:

> *Scared people often make bad decisions.*

1. **You're leaving a highly structured and predictable environment** – prison, jail, or detention center – where your daily food, housing, clothing, and medical needs were provided courtesy of taxpayers to the tune of $14,000 to $70,000 per inmate a year (nearly $70,000 a year if you are 50+ years old or $556,539 if you did jail time in New York City). Get ready for some street shocks as you move into a highly unstructured and unpredictable world that requires planning, purpose, hard work, and persistence to survive and prosper. You'll probably know within the first 90 days whether or not you're going to make it on the outside for good. Having stable housing, a good job, and convenient transportation are three good predictors of your future.

2. **Your former relationships will never be the same.** You'll be reintroducing yourself to once teary-eyed old friends and family members who may now be less than enthusiastic about seeing their long-lost loved one again. Some may try to avoid you as an "undesirable." You've lost time, and people change over time. That's life – take responsibility, learn forgiveness, suck it up, move on, and develop new relationships. There is more to life than "once-upon-a-time" friends. Most people can count really close friends on one hand. Just keep moving, and you'll eventually have a handful of good friends.

3. **You'll initially experience a mixed bag of emotions** – fear, anger, guilt, frustration, powerlessness, and impatience – that will affect your attitudes, motivations, and self-esteem, the driving forces for re-entry success. Avoid temptations to act out your negative emotions. Always remember that this is a season of your life and it, too, shall pass. Avoid making quick and impulsive decisions. Sometimes it's best to take a deep breath and simply **wait** to see what happens next. Indeed, you don't have to react to everything!

4. **Your chances of success on the outside are not good** despite whatever you may believe about your ability to succeed on the outside. At least that's what studies of recidivism continue to show for people who have been caged rather than sentenced to a rehabilitation program. But you **can** beat the discouraging

statistics if you change your mindset and patterns of behavior. That requires lots of planning and hard work, including self-motivation, self-discipline, and drive to transform your life.

5. **You are not alone when you are on your own.** While you may be reluctant to ask for assistance, you need help in the form of a support system and mentors in order to improve your chances for success. Without a support system and mentors, re-entry can be a tough road to travel. Whatever you do, don't be afraid to say "Help!" Chapter 9 focuses on "re-entry helpers."

On Your Own

Now you're on your own. You're entering a relatively unstructured and unpredictable environment that requires you to generate from $80 to $150 a day in order to survive. So start asking yourself these basic re-entry questions:

- How am I going to make it on my own and stay free? What do I do next?
- Has incarceration changed my life for the better or am I likely to repeat old patterns of behavior that got me into trouble?
- Do I have the right attitudes, motivation, drive, and skills to make it on the outside for good?
- Can I overcome the obstacles and pass the many tests for success that lie ahead?
- How can I best prepare for the challenges that lie ahead?

More specifically, you need to find answers to these important re-entry questions:

- Where will I stay?
- Do I have a firm job lined up?
- If not, how will I find employment?
- How will I get around?
- Do I have the necessary documents for life on the outside?
- Where will I get new clothes for job interviews and work?
- How can someone contact me?
- How much money will I need for the first three months out?
- Where am I going to get the money?
- Who am I going to contact for assistance?
- What new relationships should I develop?
- What old dysfunctional relationships should I avoid?
- What am I going to do for fun?

These are the questions I want to help you answer with practical how-to advice in the pages that follow. I want you to make a successful re-entry where you stay out for good and prosper in doing something very meaningful with your life. For in the end, it's in everyone's interest that you become a happy and prosperous **tax-paying citizen** rather than another angry and destitute **tax-draining prisoner**.

Don't Flunk Re-Entry 101

When you re-enter the so-called free world, you'll quickly discover that very little is free and predictable. From acquiring proper documentation, locating transitional housing, and feeding and clothing yourself to finding transportation, landing a job, establishing credit, re-establishing relationships with family members and friends, and handling new technology, the whole re-entry process is fraught with difficulties, or land mines, that can lead to rejections, disappointments, and temptations to break the law. You'll face endless barriers and seemingly impossible challenges. Not surprisingly, most ex-offenders quickly flunk the re-entry process – nearly 70 percent re-offend within three years and thus return to jail or prison. Perhaps the next time out they will do better. But don't hold your breath.

> *Freedom day for you may be **fear day** for many people on the outside.*

Precious Freedom to Create Your Future

Welcome to the world of both freedom and fear. One thing all inmates know is their **release date**. While you may have forgotten your mother's birthday or when you were last arrested or convicted, you definitely know your release date. It's really important to you, as it should be. That's Freedom Day, the day you leave the bars behind and restart your life as a free person.

It's also the day that bothers other people, who know all too well recidivism statistics and stories of ex-cons not making it on the outside. They see an ex-con coming back into their community, a freedom-starved (ex)criminal who may soon become a disruptive force. Accordingly, your **new freedom** is likely to become someone else's **new fear**.

Or is that an illusion of freedom? Let's again focus on your **choices**, for they tell us some very important things about where you are going and whether or not you will once again lose your freedom because of bad choices. If we focus on your choices, we'll understand the "real you" and perhaps specify what you need to do today to start breaking out of the vicious recidivism cycle that plagues America's vast and embarrassingly expensive and failed correctional system.

Freedom is something very precious. Indeed, for centuries people have fought and died for freedom so others can enjoy its fruits. Unfortunately, most people don't appreciate how precious freedom is until they lose it. You should know. After all, you lost your freedom. Now you have a chance to do something very special with your new freedom. If you lose it again, you have only one person to blame – yourself. In fact, you should really be angry with yourself rather than with others. Look in the mirror. It's **you** who did this to yourself. No one took away your freedom. The "system" processed you so you wouldn't mess up other people's freedom. You simply lost your freedom because of your choices. Admit it – you didn't value freedom enough to turn it into something very positive and productive. Another missed opportunity in your life.

Freedom means many things to different people. For some, it's the ability to do whatever you want to do, unconstrained by rules and regardless of consequences. Such freedom can result in unconstrained and thoughtless behaviors that trample on the freedom of others. It's a form of self-centered freedom that often results in chaos, anarchy, and criminal behavior. Many ex-offenders have been there, done that.

> *If you lose your freedom again, you have only one person to blame – yourself. You should be really angry with yourself for screwing up.*

For others, freedom is the ability to follow their dreams. It's all about making choices. This freedom allows us to set goals, decide what we want to do, think new and controversial thoughts, and decide where we want to go. Do you want to move to Denver and open a restaurant? With this freedom, you can do that if you really want to.

If we have a good job that more than pays the bills, we also have the economic freedom to do many other things, including sharing our resources with others as we build a purposeful life. With this type of freedom, you can become whatever you want to be. As such, you have the ability to shape your own future, because you understand the true potential of freedom.

Freedom also is all about **time**. It should never be wasted. As you age, you'll discover how precious time can be. It's something you can't recapture. When you lose your freedom, you also lose time with your friends and family – two of the most important ingredients in a meaningful life.

You've lost your freedom, and now you are about to regain freedom. Whatever you do, use your new freedom to create a bright future for yourself and your loved ones. You have the power to shape your future. Do it wisely by making smart choices during the first six months of your re-entry.

Your Re-Entry Success I.Q.

Let's begin by examining how well prepared you are to re-enter and succeed in the Free World. There are no right or wrong answers to the following quiz. Be aware that it is a very long and thorough exercise – it may take 30-40 minutes to complete all 149 items. Most of the issues included here will be addressed in the following chapters that correspond to a 7-step re-entry success process. The exercise is designed to give you useful feedback by measuring your current level of re-entry information, skills, and strategies as well as identifying those you need to develop and improve. Identify your level of **re-entry competence**, or how well prepared you are for re-entry, by completing the following exercise:

INSTRUCTIONS: Respond to each statement by circling which number at the right best represents your situation.

SCALE: 1 = Strongly disagree   4 = Agree
            2 = Disagree   5 = Strongly agree
            3 = Maybe, not certain

Getting Ready for Freedom Day

1. I know my release date.   1 2 3 4 5
2. I've been preparing myself for release.   1 2 3 4 5
3. I have a written re-entry plan that covers the first
   180 days after my release.   1 2 3 4 5
4. I have someone waiting to help me on the outside.   1 2 3 4 5
5. I've changed a lot for the better since I first came here.   1 2 3 4 5
6. I'm confident I can make it on the outside.   1 2 3 4 5
7. I've stayed out of trouble while incarcerated.   1 2 3 4 5

Responsibility and Forgiveness

8. I know why I'm here; I've come to terms with
   my situation.   1 2 3 4 5
9. I've taken responsibility for my actions.   1 2 3 4 5
10. I plan to never lie, make excuses, or blame others
    for my problems.   1 2 3 4 5
11. I've taken responsibility for turning my life around.   1 2 3 4 5
12. I've asked for and received forgiveness from myself
    and others.   1 2 3 4 5
13. I've decided to change my life so that I'll never
    again end up here.   1 2 3 4 5
14. I've committed myself in writing (personal contract
    spelling out what I need to do by specific dates)
    to change my life.   1 2 3 4 5
15. I usually take responsibility for my own actions
    rather than blame other people for my situation
    or circumstance.   1 2 3 4 5

Anger, Rage, and Stress

16. I seldom get angry with others.   1 2 3 4 5
17. I avoid getting into verbal or physical confrontations.   1 2 3 4 5
18. If I get angry at anyone, it's usually myself.   1 2 3 4 5
19. No one is angry with me.   1 2 3 4 5
20. I keep my stress under control.   1 2 3 4 5
21. I regularly exercise both my body and my mind.   1 2 3 4 5

Purpose and Goals

22. I believe I have a purpose in life.   1 2 3 4 5
23. I know what I both like and dislike about my life.   1 2 3 4 5
24. I try to live a purposeful life by being of value
    to others.   1 2 3 4 5
25. I volunteer to help others.   1 2 3 4 5
26. I've achieved many things in life.   1 2 3 4 5
27. I know what I want to achieve in the next 10 years.   1 2 3 4 5
28. I'm a spiritual person who acknowledges a
    higher power.   1 2 3 4 5

Character and Trustworthiness

29. I'm a person of good character.   1 2 3 4 5
30. I have high moral standards.   1 2 3 4 5
31. I usually know the difference between right and
    wrong and act accordingly.   1 2 3 4 5
32. I always tell the truth.   1 2 3 4 5
33. I'm an honest person who can be trusted.   1 2 3 4 5
34. I usually do what I say I'll do.   1 2 3 4 5
35. I've learned to trust others.   1 2 3 4 5
36. I usually see good qualities in other people.   1 2 3 4 5

Self-Esteem

37. I generally like myself and want to do good.   1 2 3 4 5
38. I feel both confident and competent in what I do.   1 2 3 4 5
39. I can laugh at myself.   1 2 3 4 5
40. I have a healthy sense of self respect.   1 2 3 4 5
41. I understand how I can be whatever I want to be.   1 2 3 4 5
42. I know I need to make some changes in my life.   1 2 3 4 5

Motivation, Self-Discipline, and Personality

43. I know what motivates me to do what I do.   1 2 3 4 5
44. I have good common sense.   1 2 3 4 5
45. I'm very well organized and use my time well.   1 2 3 4 5
46. I usually think things through before taking action.   1 2 3 4 5
47. I'm sensitive to other people's feelings.   1 2 3 4 5
48. I'm a "person of light" rather than a "person of
    heat" (see discussion on page 2).   1 2 3 4 5
49. I usually know what to do without having to be told.   1 2 3 4 5

50. I'm in better control of my impulses.   1 2 3 4 5
51. I generally have a positive attitude.   1 2 3 4 5
52. I'm not a self-centered or selfish person.   1 2 3 4 5
53. I understand my personality and how it affects others.   1 2 3 4 5

Decision-Making and Leadership

54. I consider myself to be a very mature person who
     makes good decisions for myself and others.   1 2 3 4 5
55. I'm very good at making quick and correct decisions.   1 2 3 4 5
56. Other people look up to me for advice and assistance.   1 2 3 4 5
57. I'm a team player who gets along well with others
     on the team.   1 2 3 4 5
58. I know what's right and wrong and usually try
     to do what's right.   1 2 3 4 5

Communication and Etiquette

59. I usually think before I speak.   1 2 3 4 5
60. I'm good at giving speeches before a group.   1 2 3 4 5
61. My English is very good.   1 2 3 4 5
62. I enjoy writing and I'm a good writer.   1 2 3 4 5
63. I know bad language – words, grammar, diction –
     when I hear it.   1 2 3 4 5
64. I use positive language with correct grammar
     and diction.   1 2 3 4 5
65. I avoid using rough street language.   1 2 3 4 5
66. People enjoy talking with me and listening to
     what I say.   1 2 3 4 5
67. I'm a good listener who wants to learn from others.   1 2 3 4 5
68. I have good eye contact.   1 2 3 4 5
69. I know proper etiquette, including showing up on time,
     greeting people, expressing gratitude, dressing,
     grooming, eating, and table manners.   1 2 3 4 5
70. I have a polite and likable manner; I frequently use
     the words and phrases "please," "excuse me,"
     "thank you," "would it be possible to."   1 2 3 4 5

Friends and Relationships

71. I tend to associate with people of good character.   1 2 3 4 5

72. I tend to associate with positive people and avoid
    those with negative thinking and bad language.   1 2 3 4 5
73. I tend to run with winners rather than losers.   1 2 3 4 5
74. I have many good friends.   1 2 3 4 5
75. I find it easy to make friends.   1 2 3 4 5
76. I have a few very close friends who will stand by
    me during difficult times.   1 2 3 4 5
77. I have, or can gain, the support of family and
    friends for my re-entry.   1 2 3 4 5
78. I have a mentor to help with re-entry.   1 2 3 4 5
79. I have someone waiting for me on the outside who
    will assist me with re-entry.   1 2 3 4 5
80. I get along well with authority figures.   1 2 3 4 5
81. I'm an empathetic person who has feelings for others.   1 2 3 4 5
82. I have people who love me.   1 2 3 4 5

Family

83. I come from a stable and loving family.   1 2 3 4 5
84. My relatives tend to live a long life.   1 2 3 4 5
85. I get along well with my family.   1 2 3 4 5
86. Both parents are alive and married to each other.   1 2 3 4 5
87. My family is willing to help me with re-entry.   1 2 3 4 5
88. I'm a good parent. (Don't respond if you're not a parent.)   1 2 3 4 5
89. I've been a good son or daughter.   1 2 3 4 5

Re-Entry Basics

90. I know where I'll be staying the first 90 days after release.   1 2 3 4 5
91. I don't anticipate a problem with transportation.   1 2 3 4 5
92. All my important documents are in order.   1 2 3 4 5
93. I already have a job lined up.   1 2 3 4 5
94. If I have any problems, I know where to go for help.   1 2 3 4 5
95. I have addiction or anger problems under control.   1 2 3 4 5
96. I plan to meet all my probation/parole obligations
    according to the book, including showing up on time.   1 2 3 4 5
97. I plan to avoid alcohol.   1 2 3 4 5
98. I plan to avoid drugs.   1 2 3 4 5
99. I plan to avoid people and situations that could lead
    to trouble.   1 2 3 4 5

100. I plan to never lie, make excuses, or blame others for my problems.	1 2 3 4 5
101. I am good at budgeting and saving money.	1 2 3 4 5
102. I know how to get the best deal on a car.	1 2 3 4 5

Education, Training, and Interests

103. I have my high school diploma or GED certificate.	1 2 3 4 5
104. I enjoy reading and do so frequently.	1 2 3 4 5
105. I have taken advantage of self-help programs (anger management, addiction, etc.) while incarcerated.	1 2 3 4 5
106. I've taken advantage of vocational training and skill development programs while incarcerated.	1 2 3 4 5
107. I'm eager to learn new things and acquire new skills.	1 2 3 4 5
108. I admire educated people.	1 2 3 4 5
109. I know where and how to get more education and training on the outside.	1 2 3 4 5
110. I enjoy making music – singing or playing an instrument.	1 2 3 4 5
111. I have hobbies that I enjoy and could turn into a job.	1 2 3 4 5

Mental Health and Disabilities

112. I know what's both wrong and right about me.	1 2 3 4 5
113. I seldom get depressed.	1 2 3 4 5
114. I've not received psychological counseling.	1 2 3 4 5
115. I've never been on medication for psychiatric issues.	1 2 3 4 5
116. My mental state is very good.	1 2 3 4 5
117. I'm in control of my feelings and emotions.	1 2 3 4 5
118. I'm a quick learner.	1 2 3 4 5
119. I don't experience mood swings.	1 2 3 4 5
120. I have no disabilities.	1 2 3 4 5
121. Other people feel I have my act together.	1 2 3 4 5

Jobs and Careers

122. I know what type of job or career I want to pursue.	1 2 3 4 5
123. I have the knowledge and skills to pursue that job or career.	1 2 3 4 5
124. I have a resume that clearly communicates to potential employers what I have done, can do, and will do for them in the future.	1 2 3 4 5
125. I know how to best look for jobs.	1 2 3 4 5

126. I know which jobs are best suited for ex-offenders.   1 2 3 4 5
127. I know where to look for these jobs.   1 2 3 4 5
128. I know what to say when a potential employer
     asks about my conviction and incarceration.   1 2 3 4 5
129. I can specify why employers should hire me
     despite red flags in my background.   1 2 3 4 5
130. I can list my major accomplishments.   1 2 3 4 5
131. I can develop a job referral network.   1 2 3 4 5
132. I know how to find job leads.   1 2 3 4 5
133. I can use the telephone to develop prospects and
     get referrals and interviews.   1 2 3 4 5
134. I can persuade employers to interview me.   1 2 3 4 5
135. I have a list of at least 10 questions about the
     company I want to ask during interviews.   1 2 3 4 5
136. I know the best time to talk about salary with an
     employer.   1 2 3 4 5
137. I have little difficulty in making cold calls and
     striking up conversations with strangers.   1 2 3 4 5
138. I know how to best follow up a job interview.   1 2 3 4 5
139. I would like to start my own business.   1 2 3 4 5

Dealing With Setbacks and Rejections

140. I'm generally a very positive person.   1 2 3 4 5
141. I always try to keep a positive attitude.   1 2 3 4 5
142. I approach new situations with enthusiasm.   1 2 3 4 5
143. I'm a very persistent person who does not give
     up easily.   1 2 3 4 5
144. I'm used to dealing with rejections in a positive
     manner.   1 2 3 4 5
145. I don't take rejections personally.   1 2 3 4 5
146. I'm a very resilient person who quickly bounces
     backfrom adversity.   1 2 3 4 5
147. If someone rejects me for a job, I'll be even more
     motivated to continue looking for another job.   1 2 3 4 5
148. When I get discouraged, I find strength in knowing that
     tomorrow can be a better day if only I make it happen.   1 2 3 4 5
149. I have the power within me to shape my future.   1 2 3 4 5

TOTAL _____

Calculate your potential for re-entry success by adding the numbers you circled and add them up for an overall score. If your total is less than 500 points, you need to work on developing your re-entry skills. If you score under 400, your future on the outside is likely to be tough and you may not make it for long. You need to do some serious work in preparing yourself for the Free World.

> *If your overall score is more than 600 points, you are well on your way toward re-entry success.*

In fact, how you scored each item will indicate to what degree you need to work on improving a specific indicator of re-entry success. Some things, such as changing your mindset, developing a written plan, and writing a resume, can be done immediately whereas others are things you'll need to work on over the coming months or years. After completing this book and putting many of our recommendations into practice, take this quiz again. You should now have a higher re-entry I.Q.!

If your overall score is more than 600 points, you are well on your way toward re-entry success. Focus on improving those things that appear to be re-entry weaknesses.

Activities and Exercises

The following activities and exercises are designed to get you thinking about what's really important in preparing for re-entry. I'm sure you have many questions and concerns about what comes next and whether or not you'll face barriers – either self-imposed or presented by others – to re-entry success.

1. List your 10 most important re-entry questions and/or concerns:

1. _____

2. _____

3. _____

4. _____

5. _____

6. _____

7. _____

8. _____

9. _____

10. _____

2. **What do you consider to be the most important re-entry question or concern *you* need answers to?**

    _____

    _____

    _____

3. **What do you think are the three most important questions or concerns the closest member(s) of your *family* will have concerning your release?**

    1. _____

    2. _____

    3. _____

4. **What do you think will be the three most important questions or concerns a *prospective employer* will ask about you?**

    1. _____

    2. _____

    3. _____

5. **In 75 words or less, summarize your strongest feelings (positive and/ or negative) about re-entering the Free World.**

    _____

    _____

    _____

    _____

    _____

    _____

    _____

    _____

6. **List three smart choices you've made since being incarcerated that you feel will prepare you for success on the outside.**

    1. _____

    2. _____

    3. _____

7. **List the five most important books or articles you've read during the past 12 months.**

   1. _____
   2. _____
   3. _____
   4. _____
   5. _____

8. **List the most important self-improvement classes you've attended during incarceration.**

   1. _____
   2. _____
   3. _____
   4. _____
   5. _____

9. **Summarize in no more than 100 words the *proof* you will present to employers that you have changed your life for the better.**

   _____

   _____

   _____

   _____

10. **What does freedom mean to you?**

    _____

    _____

    _____

11. **If you could change three things in your life, what would they be?**

    1. _____
    2. _____
    3. _____

12. **Where do you want to be 5 years from now?**

    _____

    _____

Wise advice everyone should live by!

"Don't be afraid to go out on a limb. That's where the fruit is."

———————

"The best preparation for tomorrow is doing your best today."

———————

"Never forget the three powerful resources you always have available to you: love, prayer, and forgiveness."

———————

Success is getting what you want. Happiness is liking what you get.

———————

When you can't change the direction of the wind, adjust your sails."

———————

Become the most positive and enthusiastic person you know.

———————

Life is slippery. Here, take my hand."

———————

Nothing is more expensive than a missed opportunity.

———————

Live your life as an exclamation, not an explanation.

———————

Never deprive someone of hope. It might be all they have.

———————

Sometimes the heart sees what is invisible to the eye.

———————

Never forget the nine most important words of any family: "I love you. You are beautiful. Please forgive me."

———————

Never underestimate your power to change yourself.

———————

*Remember that the happiest people are not those getting more,
but those giving more.*

———————

*You must take action now that will move you towards your goals.
Develop a sense of urgency in your life.*

———————

*Don't say you don't have enough time. You have exactly the same
number of hours per day that were given to Helen Keller, Louis Pasteur,
Michelangelo, Mother Teresa, Leonardo da Vinci,
Thomas Jefferson, and Albert Einstein.*

– H. Jackson Brown, Jr.
Author of *Life's Little Instruction Book*

2

Use Your Mind, Own Your Time

"Losers waste their time and mind. Winners use their time to improve their mind. Losers see tomorrow as just another day to do more time. Winners seize tomorrow as another day to exercise their mind."

WHETHER YOU ARE TECHNICALLY in what is variously called a prison, jail, detention center, or correctional facility, the reality is pretty much the same. You didn't go voluntarily; you are going to be spending more time there than you'd like; and you're not in control of your time. Unfortunately, life is short and then you get stuck doing this ostensibly useless time. Or is it really a useless way to spend time? Let's look at who actually owns your time, what you do with your time, and how you might best use it to everyone's advantage.

Owning and Using Time

When you're incarcerated, you don't own much, including your time. Some might say you're living on borrowed time! Indeed, many inmates have nothing except institutional time filled with mind-numbing rules, regulations, and procedures on what they can and can't do. There are lots of scary people here. In such an environment, it's real easy to get into trouble. You see it all around you. Indeed, time seems to stand still in prison.

> *When you own your time, it often goes fast because you keep busy doing things that most interest you.*

Since you lost your freedom, you don't control much of your time. When you own your time, it often goes fast because you keep busy doing things that most interest you. When someone else owns your time, it can go very slow and involve doing seemingly useless things of no interest to you. Indeed, time seems to stand still in prison.

Your time now belongs to the institution that requires you to do court-mandated time. Get into trouble, and you may get to do even more time and maybe even harder time. At the prison level, the "powers that be" define your time as a series of required daily routines that keep you alive, sufficiently busy, out of trouble, and maybe even focused on changing your life for the better. Such time can become psychologically oppressive. You may get angry and depressed as you cry for freedom!

You're also doing group time – you're just another number among a sea of troubling numbers that have to be locked down, secured, managed, and finally processed for the outside. As such, you're not entitled to any special time. You're still just another number.

If you learn only one thing while doing time, it's that **time is very precious**. It's something you always want to own, use wisely, and prevent others from ever taking away from you again. You can start taking ownership of your institutional time by doing certain things associated with winners.

Time and the Ex-Offender Mind

You've got lots of time on your hands. Let's face it, much of it is idle and boring time – nonproductive and mind-numbing time for those who choose to simply put in their time.

Many ex-offenders' minds are not wired for success on the outside.

Many inmates go through the five stages of grief, get angry, become negative and cynical, develop prison-speak, avoid taking chances, become manipulative, play games, dream impossible dreams, experience illusions, and resign themselves to just doing their time. Lacking a productive attitude and initiative, they settle in for the long haul and basically avoid jeopardizing their sentenced time. Some learn to "play the system" to their advantage.

Needless to say, many ex-offenders are not prepared to re-enter the fast-paced time zones of the Free World and stay there for very long. Their minds are not wired for success on the outside. Instead, their minds play the same old scenarios over again and again with similar outcomes.

As educators often say of young people, a mind is a terrible thing to lose. It's especially terrible when you choose to lose it by doing idle time. Similar to any important machine, if you don't use your mind, you'll probably lose it or see it deteriorate beyond repair. After a while, you could become delusional and go crazy with idle thoughts! Worst of all, you may become a scary ex-con with a distorted mind toward reality, especially toward people, on the outside.

Why Kill Time While Doing Time?

Most people find themselves in prison because they made poor choices. It's really that simple – lots of bad decisions made by people who should know better. Some people who go to prison persist in making poor choices and their life pattern continues. Others find entering prison to be a wake-up call and they resolve to turn their life around. No, a life change won't happen overnight. Yes, it will take time, but then again you're "doing time." In some ways prison time has a silver lining – it gives you time to make better choices and take advantage of "inside" opportunities to make progress toward a new set of goals.

What kind of bad choices/decisions have you made in your life? Maybe you dropped out of school, fell in with the wrong crowd, got hooked on drugs or alcohol, and perhaps, in order to support an alcohol or drug habit, you got involved in crime. Yes, if you did the crime, you'll have to do some time. If you did a violent crime, you'll probably do more time and have a more difficult time convincing people on the outside that doing time has changed your criminal mind and patterns of behavior.

But, unless you have a life sentence, you can take actions while you are in prison that will change and increase the opportunities available to you once you are released.

Decisions Are Forever

What are you going to do with the rest of your life? Will you become a repeat offender? Commit another crime, go through another trial or plea bargain, be sentenced and put in prison again and again – perhaps for your entire life? This is the choice some ex-offenders make – always coming home to another steel and concrete cage. Of the approximately 650,000 ex-offenders in the United States who are released from prison and re-enter life on the outside each year, nearly two-thirds are re-arrested within three years and 40 percent are sent back to prison. Such figures tell us there is something seriously wrong with both the incarceration process and the whole re-entry process. Indeed, everyone loses – you, your victims, your family, and taxpayers – when you don't make it on the outside. It's in everyone's interest to see you succeed in the Free World.

Everyone loses when you don't make it on the outside.

So you have a choice of whether you will become a repeat offender or stay clean and out of incarceration for the rest of your life. It is a choice you will make every day of your life. It is a choice you make with every action you take or resist taking. Risk going back to prison or be determined to stay out. **You** do have a choice what **you** do with **your future**. The decisions you make every day of your life impact the rest of your life.

Let's look at some hypothetical prisoners. Some of them may remind you of people you know, former friends or present inmates, or some may even seem eerily like you, yourself!

Meet Nate

Nate, to this day, still refuses to take responsibility for his actions that landed him in prison. He is not guilty. He got a bum rap. The arresting officer, the judge, the jury – everyone had it in for him. No one gave him a chance. Even his family believes he is guilty. Nate carries on in this manner to everyone around him all the time. He sounds like a broken record. The other inmates are getting tired of hearing about "poor Nate." Nate has some important "issues" he needs to deal with.

1. What do you see as Nate's problem?

_____

_____

_____

_____

2. Why will Nate's behavior keep him from moving ahead with the rest of his life?

_____

_____

_____

_____

3. What could Nate do differently that would help him move forward with his life?

_____

_____

_____

_____

True, on occasion a person who is innocent of the crime gets convicted and sent to prison. But that is the exception and not the rule. As long as Nate continues to blame everyone but himself for his "misfortune" in life, he cannot move forward. He will continue to see himself as a victim who is powerless against the other people and the system that "have it in for him." He'll begrudgingly do his time – often angry, cynical, negative, and depressed – but he's unlikely to change. Nate will leave prison older but not wiser. He'll be a good candidate for re-entry failure. Indeed, it won't take long before Nate screws up again and starts this whole sad process over again.

Meet Cory

Then there is "cool" Cory. He fell in with the wrong crowd. He never made a conscious decision to break the law, but he went along with his friends because he wanted to fit in and be accepted. So he was in the car with his friends when they were stopped for a traffic violation and the officers found illegal drugs in the car. Cory was convicted along with his friends. He is marking time in prison counting the days until his release. He believes those drugs should have been legal anyway. He also thinks he had some bad luck – in the wrong place at the wrong time. He looks forward to getting back with the "old crowd" once he gets out of prison. He's going to have some real fun celebrating his freedom. Sex, drugs, alcohol, music, and chocolate have been on his mind for a long time. In the meantime, he spends lots of time body-building, talking trash with some new buddies, and looking "cool" with his colorful but somewhat menacing body art. He met some really neat dudes on the inside who he'll keep in touch with once he's on the outside. He has been "cool" for a long time in preparation for freedom.

1. Is Cory in any way responsible for what happened to him?

_____

_____

_____

_____

2. Cory is anxious to get back with his old friends once he gets out of prison. What is likely to happen if he goes back to the "old gang"? Is this a good decision for his future?

_____

_____

_____

_____

3. How cool is Cory? Where do you think he'll go next with his life?

_____

_____

_____

_____

4. What other choices might Cory make?

_____

_____

_____

_____

Meet Marcello

Marcello didn't like school very much. He didn't do well with reading, writing, and arithmetic – especially with teachers and administrators who thought he was a loser. He felt school was a waste of his time. He couldn't see how he was ever going to make use of the subjects he was required to take in high school, so he dropped out of school and never got a diploma or a GED. Thus, he had few employment choices, and what choices he did have were limited to very low paying jobs that required lots of hard physical-work. His only other option was to go on unemployment, but he couldn't qualify for unemployment, because he hadn't been employed.

Marcello's situation gave him a lot of time with not much to do, and since he was unemployed, he always had little or no money. So crime was a major temptation. He was arrested for stealing from a local convenience store. No, you're right, he didn't get a prison sentence for petty theft. He's doing some big time, because in the process of leaving the scene of his crime, he knocked down an elderly customer who fell, hit her head, and later died in the hospital. Marcello doesn't think he's a bad guy – he just had some bad luck in that store. If that old lady would have stayed out of his way and if his mother hadn't turned him in, this all wouldn't have happened. He'd be free, having fun drinking, drugging, and doing the ladies. Marcello spends each day doing as little as possible and counts the days until he will get out and have some fun. He's got friends who will help him on the outside. Marcello thinks everything will be just fine . . . once he gets free.

1. What things could Marcello do while he is in prison that would help position him for a better future once he is released?

_____

_____

_____

_____

_____

2. How well do you think Marcello will do on the outside?

_____

_____

_____

_____

Meet Manuel

Finally, there's Manuel. He stayed in school and finished, but he did not do very well and barely managed to graduate with his class. Reading and writing were always hard for him, and he didn't enjoy them. He liked working outdoors with his hands. He took the minimum of courses required and didn't pay much attention to the electives he chose – primarily selecting classes because he thought they would be easy, or because they didn't start too early in the morning and he could sleep in later. Since there was little rhyme or reason to the classes he selected, he never developed the vocational skills he needed to get a job once he got out of school. He had few job offers, of which none held the promise of decent pay or chances for any advancement. He is spending his time in prison much like Marcello – counting the days until he will get out.

What five things would you recommend that Manuel do while in prison to help himself once he leaves prison?

1. _____

2. _____

3. _____

4. _____

5. _____

Patterns of Choice

Nate, Cory, Marcello, and Manuel each got into trouble that landed them in prison. Regardless of all the self-serving excuses they may have, no one did this to them. They are not victims of anyone or anything except their own choices. As their rap sheets clearly show, they frequently decided not to play by the rules, victimized others, and got caught. They had to be taken out of society in order to protect the public good. Their choices had consequences for themselves and others. They made choices that landed them where they are today. When they get out, they will be making choices once again that have consequences for themselves and others. The question is two-fold: What have they learned to do differently? How have they rewired their mindsets?

Choices are often cumulative – they create a distinct pathway unique to each individual.

Choices are often cumulative – they create a distinct pathway unique to each individual. Each of these inmates had made other poor choices such as not completing high school or at least getting a GED, not taking advantage of vocational training classes that would have helped them land a job, hanging out with a group of friends who were bad influences on them. They chose whether to stay in school, who they would hang out with, and what they would do with these friends. And they chose break the law and suffer the consequences. Doing the crime and doing the time go hand in hand.

Okay, so some poor choices, maybe a lot of bad decisions eventually land a person in prison. The past is over and done, and usually there is little that can be done to change past events. While some ex-offenders try to legally expunge their records, assuming such actions will give them a clean slate for re-entry, don't hold your breath. In today's high-tech society, where employers can quickly and cheaply access your record via the Internet, you really can't hide your past for long. It will eventually catch up with you. You have to look in the mirror, clean up your act, and get on with shaping what can become a wonderful life of freedom on the outside.

This time should become a **turning point** in your life. The future is yet unwritten. You can make a decision to make better choices for your future. If you are open-minded and willing to take responsibility and learn, you **can** change your life for the better!

Change Your Future

So you've got a choice. When you are released from prison, do you see it as a chance to return to your former way of life? See your old friends and hang out with them again? Are you just marking time with plans to take up life where you left off? Or can you envision yourself living a different life?

When you were a kid, what did you want to be when you grew up? Did you dream of becoming a fireman, a paramedic, an astronaut, or maybe a crime scene investi-

> *Many young people spend the first 10 years of their adult lives learning what they don't like to do.*

gator? Whatever it was, I'd bet your dream wasn't to land in prison someday. But there you are. Okay, you took a detour down some pretty bad roads, but maybe you've learned where you don't want to go. Indeed, many young people spend the first 10 years of their adult lives learning what they don't like to do. It's only after they have taken the heat that they begin to see the light and discover what they really want to do with their lives.

Hopefully, you're at that critical turning stage in your life where you know what you don't want to do in the future. You now need to make the next big step – discovering what you really want to do with your life. Accordingly, once you're out of prison you can get back on the highway headed in a new direction you want your future to take.

Two things are important at this point. First, **you** have to **want** to make the change by altering your mindset. In other words, you must be **self-motivated** and have the **drive** to change. It isn't good enough to make some lofty pie-in-the-sky promises or decide you'll make the changes because your mother wants you to, your grandmother wants you to, or your girlfriend/boyfriend, your wife or your husband wants you to do it. Deep down inside, **you have to want it for yourself**. You may want it so badly that it hurts! That's good.

Indeed, you have to believe in yourself and take ownership of your future. Once you make this critical self-transformation decision, you've made an important start toward successful re-entry to life after prison. The rest will be an action plan, lots of hard work, and persistence in the face of life's roller coaster of rejections and acceptances, disappointments and triumphs.

The second thing is to have **goals**. Your goal may be to get a job and be able to support yourself – and a family if you have one or hope to have one in the future. That is a general goal and a good enough starting point. Later you're going to need to narrow the focus a bit or make it more specific as you determine what that job is that you want to have in the future.

A job is a very important starting point – the tangible foundation on which most everything else of value in your adult life is built. A job provides money to live on as well as helps establish your credit for eventually borrowing money to buy a car, home, and other big-ticket items as well as start a business. With money you'll be able to buy life's necessities such as food, shelter, clothing, and transportation, as well as provide those things for the significant others in your life – your family.

Tooling Up for Release

I focus exclusively on the "how to" of the job search in my companion volume, ***The Ex-Offender's Quick Job Hunting Guide***. You can't have a successful job search unless you have the **tools** to land the right job and keep it once you've got it. The tools I'm talking about here include making decisions and setting goals, dealing with obstacles and overcoming barriers to achieving your goals, getting the education/training and relevant skill set, gaining work experience, and making contacts and maintaining a network of potential references. Yes, believe it or not, you can do all these things while you are in prison. You don't have to wait until you get out to get started on the rest of your life. In fact, if you use your time in prison wisely, you can position yourself to be at the "starting gate" on the day you are released.

What's in Your Future?

What do you see in your future as you look ahead five years, ten years, or more? Right now you're probably looking forward to the day you'll get out of prison, but then what? After the euphoria of being back on the outside, the hard reality sets in. What will you do? Where will you live? Do you have a supportive family? Who will your friends likely be? What will you do with your time?

Right now, many decisions are made for you. How well will you cope when you are free to make decisions for yourself? Do you see yourself being out of prison for a while and then returning to prison one or more times? That's what happens to a lot of inmates, or, rather, that is what a lot of inmates do to themselves. In other words, prison doesn't just happen; you generally do something to put yourself in prison. By not planning for the future, ex-offenders let life happen to them rather than trying to shape the life they would like to live.

I don't promise you magic. I don't tell you it will be easy. What I do tell you is that **you can shape your future** to a large extent. Not only that, but you can begin to do it now. In fact, you need to start now. As the old adage says, *"Today is the first day of the rest of your life."* You will be much better prepared to take charge of your life rather than letting life happen to you if you take steps now to prepare for the day when you are on your own again.

Survival Skills for Life

I'm going to ask you to respond to a few statements about yourself. The statements are easy in a way, because only you can determine the response, and since they are about you, no one else can tell you your responses are wrong. The hard part is that the statements require you to be honest with yourself if you are to gain insight into your knowledge, skills, and motivations.

Mark each statement using the following key:

> 1 = Yes   4 = Not really
> 2 = Sort of   5 = No
> 3 = Maybe

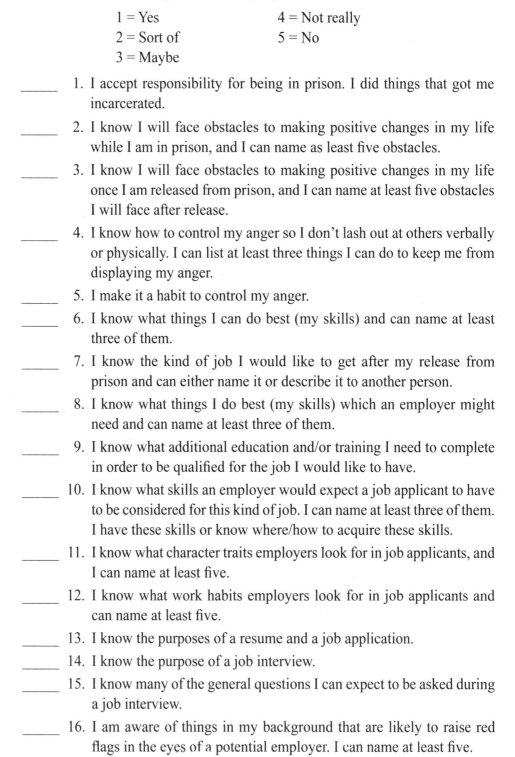

_____   1. I accept responsibility for being in prison. I did things that got me incarcerated.

_____   2. I know I will face obstacles to making positive changes in my life while I am in prison, and I can name as least five obstacles.

_____   3. I know I will face obstacles to making positive changes in my life once I am released from prison, and I can name at least five obstacles I will face after release.

_____   4. I know how to control my anger so I don't lash out at others verbally or physically. I can list at least three things I can do to keep me from displaying my anger.

_____   5. I make it a habit to control my anger.

_____   6. I know what things I can do best (my skills) and can name at least three of them.

_____   7. I know the kind of job I would like to get after my release from prison and can either name it or describe it to another person.

_____   8. I know what things I do best (my skills) which an employer might need and can name at least three of them.

_____   9. I know what additional education and/or training I need to complete in order to be qualified for the job I would like to have.

_____   10. I know what skills an employer would expect a job applicant to have to be considered for this kind of job. I can name at least three of them. I have these skills or know where/how to acquire these skills.

_____   11. I know what character traits employers look for in job applicants, and I can name at least five.

_____   12. I know what work habits employers look for in job applicants and can name at least five.

_____   13. I know the purposes of a resume and a job application.

_____   14. I know the purpose of a job interview.

_____   15. I know many of the general questions I can expect to be asked during a job interview.

_____   16. I am aware of things in my background that are likely to raise red flags in the eyes of a potential employer. I can name at least five.

_____ 17. I know what to say on my resume or on a job application about the time I have spent in prison.

_____ 18. I know what to say in a job interview to make the employer feel more comfortable about hiring a person who has been incarcerated and about problem behaviors from my past. I can name at least three ways I could deal with this.

_____ 19. I know there are things I can do between now and my release from prison to show an employer that the problems/behaviors of my past will not re-occur. I can name at least three things I can do.

_____ 20. I know how to respond to questions about the red flags in my past.

_____ 21. If the employer does not ask, I know how to bring up questionable areas of my past so I can deal in a positive way with the employer's unspoken concerns.

_____ 22. I know what to expect as conditions of my eventual parole/release.

_____ 23. I know what jobs I cannot hold as a result of my incarceration.

_____ 24. I have/will be able to find housing once I am released.

_____ 25. I know what organizations in my community can provide assistance and what kinds of assistance I can expect.

_____ 26. I know how to make a budget.

_____ 27. I have the resolve to stick to a budget.

The purpose of responding to these 27 statements is not to get a score, because it's not really a test – it's a tool. Its purpose is to get you to think about the issues to cover: accepting responsibility for your past actions, considering your goals, what you will need to know or do to achieve your goals, and some of the obstacles you will face both in prison and once you are released. These will be topics of discussion through the rest of this book.

Change Your Mindset

Certain things you **can't change** – your age, race, birthplace, parents. Other things you **can change** – knowledge, skills, relationships, education, residence, jobs, transportation, credit rating, thinking, hair color, body art, health, clothes, habits, patterns of behavior. Your rap sheet is something you'll have difficulty changing – there's nowhere to hide in today's high-tech tracking society – but you can offset its negatives with other behaviors you can change.

Throughout life it's important to know what it is you can and can't change and act accordingly.

Throughout life it's important to know what it is you **can and can't change** and act accordingly. It's also important to separate **illusions from reality** and be aware of important **seasons in life**. When you don't change things you can change, it means you've simply decided to continue doing what you've always done. Not surprisingly, the consequences of doing the same things over and over again will most likely be the same. Indeed, the old definition of **insanity** as *"doing the same thing over and over again in expectation of getting a different result"* is especially relevant to ex-offenders who often become **repeat offenders**. Yes, being a repeat offender is a form of insanity!

In fact, if you take an inventory of things you can and can't change, you'll quickly discover that there are many things you **can** change about your life. While you may encounter some barriers to making changes, nonetheless, you can make many changes in your life if you decide you really want to make those changes. Whatever you do, don't make **excuses** for not making changes that are within your power to make. Making excuses is just another way of saying you don't have the willpower to change your life.

Changes that will really make a difference in your life must come from **within you**, which means inside your **head**. Are you wired for success in the next phase of your life or do you just sit around angry, replay old scenarios, and complain about your past and present? Can you think outside the box or are you stuck in a box that continues to drag you down and propel you into a scary and uncertain future? How do you view your situation, your prison world, and the Free World? How do you approach your life and others?

Making changes is all about your mindset – how you think about yourself and others as well as act toward the world around you. It's about making changes in your beliefs and attitudes. What you think **does** have an impact on what you do today and tomorrow. Change your thinking, or brain or mindset, and you can change your life.

The best way to illustrate your mindset is to examine these two contrasting views of one's incarceration:

Situation #1 – Thinking Inside the Depressing Box

I've been convicted and sentenced. I can't believe this has happened to me. Maybe I made a few mistakes, but I don't deserve being locked up with all these losers. I've hit bottom and I don't know what to do – I'm so frightened, depressed, and bored. I may not make it. With my record, I'll be damaged goods for the rest of my life. No one will want to hire or help me. Yes, I should have done some things differently. But now my life is ruined. Sometimes I just want to die. I'm scared about my life here as well as what's going to happen to me in the future.

Situation #2 – Thinking Outside the Same Box

I've been convicted and sentenced to two years in this place. It's not pretty, but things could be worse – I could be dead! While I could have done things differently, nonetheless, I'm here and I'm going to make the best of this situation. The good news is that I have lots of time to think, read, attend classes, and plan for the future – more such time than I'll ever have again. I'm not a loser, and I'm not going to let this place kill my spirit. I'm going to set some new goals – short-, intermediate-, and long-range – and see what I can learn that will help me on the outside. In fact, I'm going to turn this place into a new opportunity to truly change my life for the better. I'm actually looking forward to the next two years. I'm really going to make something of myself here. First, I'm going to see the psychologist next week and ask him to help me put together a two-year plan to turn my life around. Second, tomorrow I'm heading to the prison library to get some self-help books. Third . . .

Which of these two situations most closely approximates your initial approach toward your incarceration?

_____ Situation #1   _____ Situation #2

Why did you choose to think that way?

_____

_____

_____

_____

_____

Let's face it; no one is happy about being locked up with a group of convicted criminals who think they have to be physically tough to survive and prosper. That mindset probably got them into trouble to begin with! But what's really important is how you mentally get up when you're down – what you plan to do with your life, your dreams and goals, rather than what others may do to you and how you're going to handle them. Life at times is tough, but you have to get up, dust yourself off, and move ahead with your head screwed on straight and pointed in the right direction for long-term success.

In other words, you need to **take charge of your future** by shaping that future first in your mind and then outside your cell and on the street. In fact, you may want to make today the first day of your new life by changing your mindset about your current situation and your future!

Referring to the two contrasting examples above, now tell me your story during the first 3-12 months of your incarceration:

1. **How did you approach (or what were you thinking about during) the first few months of your incarceration?**

_____

_____

_____

_____

_____

_____

2. What was your thinking about your future?

_____

_____

_____

_____

_____

3. What specifically did you do to prepare yourself for the Free World?

_____

_____

_____

_____

_____

_____

View Prison as an Opportunity

An opportunity you may scoff, "I don't want to be here, but I don't have a choice. I'd rather be almost any place but here."

Is your glass half empty or half full? How you perceive your current situation makes a difference in how you deal with today and tomorrow. Look at it this way. The public spends somewhere between $25,000 and $500,000 to keep you safe from yourself and others and to ensure that you don't generate an income for paying taxes. Keeping you in a cage and out of public sight is VERY expensive. Here's what taxpayers pay for: Your housing is being provided; no matter how bad the food, your meals are provided as well; you don't have to worry about transportation or even your medical care. Turn the negatives in your situation around to see that there are actually some positives that you can make work for you. Adjust your viewpoint to "accentuate the positives" as the children's song goes.

Ok, let's get started on your future. You have a big part to play in this because only **you** can decide what you want out of life, and only **you** can make it happen. There will be a lot of people and organizations that will be ready, willing, and able to help you, but you have to take control of your future.

What Do You Want to Be When You Grow Up?

This is a legitimate question for you to ask yourself – no matter what your age is – whether you are 16 or 60. You can determine your future at any age, and sometimes as we age we find that our goals for our lives change. Don't be afraid to decide you have different goals today than you had a few months or years ago.

1. **If there were no limitations on what you could be or do, what would you do with your life?**

   _____

   _____

   _____

   _____

2. **If you were told that someone had deposited unlimited funds in a bank account in your name, but that money could only be spent on education or training for a job or career, what training courses or educational degrees would you sign up for?**

   _____

   _____

   _____

   _____

3. **A second bank account has been set up in your name with unlimited funds, but the money in this account can only be used for personal enrichment courses or counseling. For example, you could spend money from this account for psychological testing, counseling for personal growth or personal problems, family counseling to deal with problems with family members, rehabilitation for addictive behavior(s), classes at the local community college related to a hobby you would like to pursue (but not job related), or even to hire a personal trainer at a nearby athletic club. How would you spend this money?**

   _____

   _____

   _____

   _____

4. **Yet another bank account has been set up in your name. But this account does not come with a deposit of unlimited funds. Your benefactor has deposited $2,000. In this account. The money will earn interest until your release from prison. At the time of your release you will be handed the money in this account in cash. What will you do with this money?**

   _____

   _____

   _____

5. **While you are serving your time in prison, your benefactor notices that you are being a "model" prisoner. You have "owned up" to the crimes you committed, followed the rules while you were in prison, taken classes to further your education, worked part-time on the prison highway crew to earn some money as well as obtain a job reference that will be useful when you are released, and you participated in anger management sessions. Since you have led such an exemplary life while you were in prison, your benefactor decides to increase the money you will be given upon release to $5,000. What will you do with this money?**

_____

_____

_____

_____

_____

_____

_____

Even though the above scenarios you responded to were fictitious, your responses to the questions may help you form realistic goals for your future. Was your response to #1 something you could reasonably see yourself actually achieving? If so, that's great. You can incorporate that into one of the most important re-entry success steps – setting achievable goals. If it isn't really likely to happen, you will have a chance to see whether it helps you focus on a related goal that may actually be achievable.

Your response to #2 may have been more ambitious than your bank account will allow at present, but a piece of it might be achievable now and the rest might be achievable in the future. Some goals take time to reach.

Question #3 gave you a chance to think about personal development issues that go beyond training or education for a job. Some counseling is usually available within prison. See what is available and seek out ways to get help now if needed, so you are less likely to have to pay for it later.

Your responses to #4 and #5 indicate a lot about how realistic you are about handling money. Assuming you are not independently wealthy and won't have much, if any other, money available to you upon your release, I certainly hope you didn't decide to take that $5,000 and go out and buy a car. Once you are released you will suddenly have to start paying for a lot of things that have been provided for you while you were in prison. These basics include food, housing, transportation, and medical services. It may take some time to land a job. The best course of action with either $2,000 or $5,000 would be to hang onto it for your future necessary expenses.

3

7 Steps to True Freedom

"True freedom is when you own your own time and space. It enables you to make smart choices to further expand your time and space."

RE-ENTRY SUCCESS IS ALL ABOUT achieving true freedom – **the ability to own your own time and space**. With true freedom, nothing can hold you back from expanding your time and space. While you may encounter obstacles or barriers along the way, with true freedom you can be whatever you want to be – and serve whoever you want to serve. As you'll see in subsequent chapters, you can achieve true freedom if you do certain things between now and the day you are released. You'll need to focus on those things about your life that are within your power to change. If you'll earnestly focus on creating a new you, you'll soon taste the joys of true freedom.

What's Wrong With You?

As many successful people will tell you, there's nothing magical about achieving success in life. While some people had good luck, most share a common thread – the **drive to succeed**. They discovered within themselves the ability to shape their future according to their dreams and beyond. Above all, their minds are wired for success. They think and behave differently from others.

So what's your problem? Why can't you get it together while the rest of the world is passing you by? What's wrong with you? What's your purpose in life? What do you want to do before you die?

Perhaps there's nothing really wrong with you – it's just not your time to become the best person you can be. Maybe you've taken a temporary detour off a path that's destined to lead you elsewhere with your life. After all, we all have seasons in life. Nothing is forever, and this too will pass. Did you know, for example, that Colonel Harland Sanders of Kentucky Fried Chicken (KFC) fame didn't get started in the fabulously successful chicken business until after age 65? He was the ultimate late bloomer!

Create Your Own Season

Just think about it for a moment. Perhaps this is your season to start something new and exciting with your life. So what do you plan to do next? Will you keep following the same old path that brought you here or do you see another way ahead?

Answer the following questions about yourself as truthfully as possible. There are no right or wrong answers – just responses that will help you better plan your re-entry future.

1. What path have you chosen thus far in your life?

_____

_____

_____

_____

2. What do you like and dislike about your life?

Likes	Dislikes
_____	_____
_____	_____
_____	_____
_____	_____
_____	_____

3. What path do you see ahead for you during the next 10 years?

_____

_____

_____

_____

4. If you could be anything you wanted to be, what would it be?

_____

_____

_____

_____

5. On a scale from 1 to 10, what do you see as your probability of becoming what you want to be? (Circle a number that best represents your probability)

1	2	3	4	5	6	7	8	9	10
Little probability									Very high probability

6. What five things do you need to do to become what you want to be?

1. _____

2. _____

3. _____

4. _____

5. _____

What Do You Want to Be, Who Do You Want to Serve?

As people grow older and wiser, they often make a distinction between **being** and **serving**. When you were a child, people asked you what you wanted to be when you grow up. This notion of "being something" is a very self-centered idea – it focuses on you as the individual. It's all about looking in the mirror and developing a strong self-concept of being something. Maybe you want to be macho, sexy, rich, respected, educated, a mechanic, a stockbroker, or something else related to a job or career. To be "something" fits nicely into a material-oriented culture that emphasizes the importance of being rich and accumulating lots of stuff. In such a "me, me, me" culture, ex-offenders re-entering society have to learn how to survive economically. They face pressure to get a good job and develop a clean record that qualifies them for credit so they can start accumulating the normal stuff (house, cars, TVs, computers) associated with living in a materialistic culture.

On the other hand, some people are born to **serve** others – to help their fellow man and be good stewards. These people want to be useful to others, to make this world a better place for their children and others. These are the heroes of society, the ones who sacrifice their own well-being for the larger good. Disproportionately associated with faith-based and nonprofit organizations, these people get great satisfaction in giving to others.

I'll re-address this issue when I discuss your **purpose** (Chapter 5) in life and the importance of leaving a **legacy** (Chapter 10). In the meantime, what exactly do you want to be and who do you want to serve in the next phase of your life? How can you get the two to come together – satisfy both your needs and contribute to the well-being of others?

7 Steps to a New Life

Remember the commercial with the stumbling and aging actor who cries out *"I've fallen and I can't get up"*? The most important part of that commercial is this – the person recognizes that he or she has fallen and needs help! And help will be on the way if they only purchase that little electronic device that broadcasts their dire situation to those who are in a position to help them stand up on their own again . . . until they fall again.

Well, you're not being issued a remote device that brings on a 911 rescue squad every time you fall down. If you've fallen and you've decided you won't take the necessary action to get up and stay up (or worse still, you don't realize you've actually fallen!), expect to stay down for a long time. You'll soon be treated like human trash.

While some people may try to help you get back on your feet, you have to do a lot of work to make sure you don't keep falling again and again and telling the same old *"I'm really going to change this time"* story. After a while, no one will want to pick you up again and put you on your feet. You must take care of yourself by following a new path to success based upon new attitudes, motivations, and drive.

If you've ever gone through a substance abuse rehab and recovery program, you know how difficult it is to make changes and avoid relapse. Indeed, temptations to abuse your mind (drugs, pornography, anger) and body (alcohol, tobacco, sugar) – both legal and illegal – abound in the Free World. Try as hard as you may to kick habits, relapse is very easy. If you've gone through a 12-step AA or NA program, or an anger management program, you know how important it is to be honest with yourself and others, take responsibility, and admit that you have a problem requiring intervention and behavioral modification.

Frequently falling into relapse, few people with addiction problems ever make permanent changes in their thinking and behavior. But they have to start with being honest with themselves. For if you're not honest with yourself, you're just fooling yourself that you're prepared to transform your life and develop a new path to self-renewal.

The 7 steps for re-entry success, or what I call "true freedom," outlined throughout this book are ones that you may have heard about before but never internalized as part of your day-to-day attitudes and behavior. They've not become recurring **habits** – things you do without having to think about them all the time. These include the following steps:

1. Change your attitudes and motivations. **(Chapter 4)**
2. Develop a purpose and plan in your life. **(Chapter 5)**
3. Get smart through education, training, and lifelong learning. **(Chapter 6)**
4. Tell a true and compelling story about the new you. **(Chapter 7)**
5. Take responsibility and build trust. **(Chapter 8)**
6. Seek assistance for lifelong recovery. **(Chapter 9)**
7. Leave a legacy by being a good friend, spouse, parent, and citizen. **(Chapter 10)**

The remaining chapters of this book examine each of these 7 steps. Each chapter includes exercises for both better understanding the step and internalizing it as part of your re-entry success plan. If you complete each of these chapters, you should be better prepared to achieve true freedom on the outside. You'll begin creating a future that will be extremely rewarding in the years ahead. You'll never again lose your freedom because you failed to take care of yourself and those around you. Best of all, when you own your time, you'll be able to expand your space!

7 Steps to Freedom in the Outside World

7. Leave a legacy by being a good friend, spouse, parent, and citizen. (Chapter 10)

6. Seek assistance for lifelong recovery. (Chapter 9)

5. Take responsibility and build trust. (Chapter 8)

4. Tell a true and compelling story about the new you. (Chapter 7)

3. Get smart through education, training, and lifelong learning. (Chapter 6)

2. Develop a purpose in your life. (Chapter 5)

1. Change your attitudes and motivation. (Chapter 4)

4

Change Your Attitudes and Motivations

"Attitude is the key to success. Like a laser, it directs everything you do.
The secret to changing your life is to first change your attitude."

WHAT KIND OF PEOPLE do you admire – positive or negative? What type of people do you attract – winners or losers? Are you generally a positive or negative person in what you think, say, and do? Do you often get angry and express your anger in what you say and do? Do you frequently use such negative and depressing terms as "can't," "don't," or "won't" when talking about yourself and others, or do you use positive terms such as "can," "will," or "should"? What motivates you to do your very best? What do you really know about your attitudes and motivations? How do they guide your behavior? When was the last time you had an attitude check-up as well as a motivation tune-up?

Something You Can Change Now

Unlike your age, sex, race, and rap sheet, your attitudes and motivations are things you can **change now** – not next week, next month, or next year. Right now. But first you need to meet the real you by becoming better acquainted with your attitudes and motivations. If your attitudes and motivations are affected by deep-seated anger and depression issues, you may need professional help to better manage your anger and overcome recurring depression. If your attitudes and motivations also are clouded by addiction issue, you definitely need to seek help rather than try to deal with these issues on your own.

Let's do an attitude and motivation check-up to see if we need a tune-up or a major overhaul in creating a new you for re-entry success.

Attitude May Be Your Best Asset

Few ex-offenders have an infectious positive, can-do attitude. Many feel worthless, hopeless, and unwanted. Their negative attitudes are often obvious to family, friends, and employers. They use a depressive vocabulary. Not surprisingly, those attitudes affect their motivation in getting ahead, be it developing new relationships, finding and keeping a job, getting promoted, acquiring a loan, finding housing, or maintaining a marriage or other important relationships. Indeed, their attitude often gets them into trouble. Many might be best called "serial attitude offenders" who sabotage themselves. Frankly, no one wants to hang around people who have an attitude problem. No one wants to give you a job or keep you on the job if you have bad attitudes.

> *Your attitude may well become your most important asset for re-entry success.*

Your attitude may well become your most important asset for re-entry success. However, your re-entry will probably be filled with anxiety and uncertainty – uncertain how people will receive you, uncertain about your family, uncertain about your housing and financial situations, and uncertain whether or not you will find a job and succeed on the outside. If you harbor anger and negative attitudes, chances are you also lack the necessary motivation to become successful. If you are an older ex-offender, who may have been incarcerated for several years, you may be especially fearful of re-entering the job market and society. Unlike many young offenders, older ex-offenders often lack **self-motivation skills** that are essential for success.

What's Your Attitude?

If you have nothing to start with, at least you have an attitude that will potentially motivate you and thus propel you to success. On the other hand, your attitude might drag you down a road to failure. Take a moment to examine your attitude. Is it negative much of the time? Do you often make excuses? Does your attitude show in what you say and do? Are others attracted to you in a positive manner? What motivates you to succeed?

One of the first things you need to do is check the state of your attitude. You can do this by completing the following exercise. Check whether or not you primarily agree ("Yes") or disagree ("No") with each of these statements:

	Yes	No
1. Other people often make my work and life difficult.	❏	❏
2. When I get into trouble, it's often because of what someone else did rather than my fault.	❏	❏
3. People often take advantage of me.	❏	❏
4. When I worked, people less qualified than me often got promoted.	❏	❏
5. I avoid taking risks because I'm afraid of failing.	❏	❏
6. I don't trust many people.	❏	❏
7. Not many people trust me.	❏	❏
8. Not many people I know take responsibility.	❏	❏
9. Most people get ahead because of connections, schmoozing, and politics.	❏	❏

10. When I worked, I was assigned more duties than other people in similar positions. ❑ ❑

11. I expect to be discriminated against in the job search and on the job. ❑ ❑

12. I don't feel like I can change many things; I've been dealt this hand, so I'll have to live with it. ❑ ❑

13. I've had my share of bad luck. ❑ ❑

14. I usually have to do things myself rather than rely on others to get things done. ❑ ❑

15. People often pick on me. ❑ ❑

16. Employers try to take advantage of job seekers by offering them low salaries. ❑ ❑

17. I don't like many of the people I have worked with. ❑ ❑

18. There's not much I can do to get ahead. ❑ ❑

19. My ideas are not really taken seriously. ❑ ❑

20. I often think of reasons why other people's ideas won't work. ❑ ❑

21. I sometimes respond to suggestions by saying *"Yes, but...,"* *"I'm not sure...,"* *"I don't think it will work...,"* *"Let's not do that..."* ❑ ❑

22. Other people are often wrong, but I have to put up with them nonetheless. ❑ ❑

23. I don't see why I need to get more education and training. ❑ ❑

24. I often wish other people would just disappear. ❑ ❑

25. I sometimes feel depressed. ❑ ❑

26. I have a hard time getting and staying motivated. ❑ ❑

27. I don't look forward to going to work. ❑ ❑

28. Friday is my favorite workday. ❑ ❑

29. When I worked, I sometimes came to work late or left early. ❑ ❑

30. The jobs I've had didn't reflect my true talents. ❑ ❑

31. I should have advanced a lot further than where I am today. ❑ ❑

32. I'm worth a lot more than most employers are willing to pay. ❑ ❑

33. I've been known to do things behind my boss's back that could get me into trouble ❑ ❑

TOTALS _____ _____

Not all of these statements necessarily reflect bad attitudes or negative behaviors. Some may accurately reflect realities you encounter. In fact, some organizations breed negative attitudes and behaviors among their employees. However, if you checked "Yes" to more than six of these statements, you may be harboring some bad attitudes that could negatively affect your re-entry, especially when looking for a job and performing on the job. You may want to examine these attitudes as possible **barriers to getting ahead** in the Free World. Indeed, you may want to change those attitudes that may be preventing you from making good choices and getting ahead.

Examples of Attitudes I Need to Change

1. _____
2. _____
3. _____
4. _____
5. _____

I Will Change These Attitudes By Doing the Following

_____

_____

_____

_____

What Excuses Do You Make?

Many negative attitudes are related to excuses we make for our behavior. Take, for example, the following list of "100 Excuses for Choosing Poor Behavior" compiled by Rory Donaldson. While many of these excuses apply to school children, many also relate to everyone else. He prefaces this list with Rudyard Kipling's observation that *"We have forty million reasons for failure, but not a single excuse."*

1. It's your fault.
2. I'm not happy.
3. It's too hot.
4. I'm too busy.
5. I'm sad.
6. I didn't sleep well.
7. It's not fair.
8. I wanted to watch TV.
9. I didn't write it down.
10. It's too hard.
11. It's too far away.
12. The teacher didn't explain it.
13. I forgot.
14. The dog was sick.
15. There was too much traffic.
16. I tried.
17. My pencil broke.
18. My grandmother wouldn't let me.
19. You're mean.
20. I didn't know it was today.

21. I'm too tired.
22. My brother was sick.
23. The car broke down.
24. It was snowing.
25. I hurt my foot.
26. I thought it was due tomorrow.
27. The ice was too thin.
28. I ran out of time.
29. I hurt my finger.
30. I don't feel well.
31. You didn't tell me.
32. It was cold.
33. I'm not good at that.
34. I left it in my pocket.
35. He made a face at me.
36. I wasn't.
37. I was rushed.
38. You didn't give it to me.
39. We did that last year.
40. That's not the way we learned at school.
41. His mother said it was O.K.
42. I already did it.
43. It was right here.
44. It's too much work.
45. It stinks.
46. I didn't know it was sharp.
47. I was scared.
48. I was frustrated.
49. I did already.
50. It wasn't in the dictionary.
51. I lost it.
52. Nobody likes me.
53. I have poor self esteem.
54. I'm too happy.
55. I'm sleepy.
56. He hit me.
57. I already know that.
58. I left it at school.
59. It's too easy.
60. It's not important.
61. I couldn't get into my locker.
62. I dropped it.
63. I have a learning disorder.
64. I lost my pencil.
65. My pen leaked.
66. I have an excuse.
67. It got wet.
68. It got dirty.
69. My dog threw up.
70. I missed the bus.
71. I have a different learning style.
72. It was raining.
73. My grandfather was visiting.
74. I didn't know.
75. No one told me.
76. I don't have to.
77. My neck hurts.
78. I ran out of paper.
79. The electricity went out.
80. I don't know how.
81. I can't.
82. I don't know where it is.
83. He hit me first.
84. It's the weekend.
85. I ran out of money.
86. I'm too stupid.
87. My teacher said to do it this way.
88. I watched it at my friend's house.
89. I just cleaned it.
90. My friend got one.
91. You lost it.
92. It takes too much time.
93. He told me I didn't have to.
94. I'm hungry.
95. I couldn't open the door.
96. I'm too important.
97. It spilled.
98. I ran out of batteries.
99. I'm doing something else.
100. I didn't know it was hot.

I and other employers have often encountered 25 additional excuses related to the workplace. Some are even used by candidates during a job interview to explain their on-the-job behavior! Most of these excuses reflect an attitude lacking in truthfulness, responsibility, and initiative:

1. No one told me.
2. I did what you said.
3. Your directions were bad.
4. It's not my fault.
5. She did it.
6. It just seemed to happen.
7. It happens a lot.
8. What did he say?
9. I had a headache.
10. I don't understand why.
11. I don't know how to do it.
12. That's your problem.
13. It wasn't very good.
14. Maybe you did it.
15. I thought I wrote it down.
16. That's not my style.
17. He told me to do it that way.
18. I've got to go now.
19. Where do you think it went?
20. We can talk about it later.
21. My computer crashed.
22. The Internet went down.
23. I think someone gave me a virus.
24. I didn't get your email. Where did you send it?
25. My prayers weren't answered.

We all make excuses. Many are harmless excuses that help us get through the day. Identify a few excuses you frequently make:

1. _____
2. _____
3. _____
4. _____
5. _____

On the other hand, certain excuses may prevent you from getting and keeping a job. Identify any excuses you make that may work against finding and keeping a job:

1. _____
2. _____
3. _____
4. _____
5. _____

When you express such excuses, you literally **show an attitude** that is not appreciated by employers. People with positive attitudes and proactive behavior do not engage in behaviors that reflect such excuses. They have a "can do" attitude that helps focus their minds on doing those things that are most important to achieving their goals. For example, rather than show up 10 minutes late for a job interview and say they got lost or had bad directions, people with positive attitudes and proactive behavior check out the interview location the day before in anticipation of arriving 10 minutes early. They make no excuses because they plan ahead and engage in no-excuses behavior!

Does Your Attitude Indicate Red Flags?

Much of re-entry success involves making good first impressions on strangers who know little or nothing about your background and capabilities. This is especially true when looking for a job. Whether you are completing an application, writing a resume, or interviewing for a job, your attitude will show in many different ways, both verbally and nonverbally.

Many job seekers show attitudes of disrespect, deceit, laziness, irresponsibility, and carelessness – all **red flags** that will quickly eliminate you from the competition. Most of these attitudes are communicated during the critical job interview when employers have a chance to read both verbal and nonverbal behavioral cues. Here are some common mistakes job seekers make that show off some **killer attitudes** that also reflect on their character:

Mistake	Attitude/Character
▪ Lacks a job objective	Confused and unfocused
▪ Misspells words on application, resume, and letters	Careless and uneducated
▪ Uses poor grammar	Uneducated
▪ Sends resume to the wrong person	Careless and error-prone
▪ Arrives late for the job interview	Unreliable and inconsiderate
▪ Dresses inappropriately	Unperceptive and insensitive
▪ Doesn't know about the company	Lazy and thoughtless
▪ Talks about salary and benefits	Greedy and self-centered
▪ Bad-mouths previous employer	Disrespectful and angry
▪ Doesn't admit to any weaknesses	Disingenuous and calculating
▪ Boasts about himself/herself	Obnoxious, self-centered, and narcissistic
▪ Lies about background	Deceitful
▪ Lacks eye contact	Shifty and dishonest
▪ Blames others for problems	Irresponsible
▪ Interrupts and argues	Inconsiderate and impatient
▪ Has trouble answering questions	Unprepared and nervous
▪ Fails to ask any questions	Uninterested in job
▪ Jumps from one extreme to another	Manic and unfocused
▪ Fails to close and follow up interview	Doesn't care about the job

On the other hand, employers look for attitudes that indicate a candidate has some of the following **positive characteristics**:

- Accurate
- Adaptable
- Careful
- Competent
- Considerate
- Cooperative
- Dependable
- Determined
- Diligent
- Discreet
- Driven
- Educated
- Efficient
- Empathic
- Energetic
- Enthusiastic
- Fair
- Focused
- Good-natured
- Happy
- Helpful
- Honest
- Intelligent
- Loyal
- Nice
- Open-minded
- Patient
- Perceptive
- Precise
- Predictable
- Prompt
- Purposeful
- Reliable
- Resourceful
- Respectful
- Responsible
- Self-motivated
- Sensitive
- Sincere
- Skilled
- Tactful
- Team player
- Tenacious
- Tolerant
- Trustworthy
- Warm

Your attitudes will also affect other important re-entry activities, such as finding housing, establishing credit, and obtaining assistance. All of these activities involve interacting with strangers who will draw conclusions about your character based upon how they respond to your attitude.

Change Your Attitudes

If you have negative attitudes and often need to make excuses for your behavior, you are probably an unhappy person. It's time you took control of both your attitudes and behaviors. Start by identifying several of your negative attitudes and try to transform them into positive attitudes. As you do this, you will begin to identify the positive-minded person you want to be. For starters, examine these sets of negative and positive attitudes that can arise at various stages of the job search, especially during the critical job interview:

- Negative Attitude	+ Positive Attitude
- I've just gotten out of prison and need a job.	+ While incarcerated, I turned my life around by getting my GED, learning new skills, and controlling my anger. I'm really excited about becoming a landscape architect and working with your company.
- I didn't like my last employer.	+ It was time for me to move on to a more progressive company.

- I haven't been able to find a job in over three months. I really want this one.

+ I've been learning a great deal during the past several weeks of my job search.

- My last two jobs were problems.

+ I learned a great deal about what I really love to do from those last two jobs.

- Do you have a job for me?

+ I'm in the process of conducting a job search. Do you know anyone who might have an interest in someone with my qualifications?

- I can't come in for an interview tomorrow since I'm interviewing for another job. What about Wednesday? That looks good.

+ I have a conflict tomorrow. Wednesday would be good. Could we do something in the morning?

- Yes, I flunked out of college in my sophomore year.

+ After two years in college I decided to pursue a career in computer sales.

- I really hated studying math.

+ Does this job require math?

- Sorry about that spelling error on my resume. I was never good at spelling.

+ (Doesn't point it out; if the interviewer asked, replied *"It's one that got away."*)

- I don't enjoy working in teams.

+ I work best when given an assignment that allows me to work on my own.

- What does this job pay?

+ How does the pay scale here compare with other firms in the area?

- Will I have to work weekends?

+ What are the normal hours for someone in this position?

- I have to see my parole officer once a month. Can I have that day off?

+ I have an appointment I need to keep the last Friday of each month. Would it be okay if I took off three hours that day?

- I'm three months pregnant. Will your health care program cover my delivery?

+ Could you tell me more about your benefits, such as health and dental care?

Can you think of any particular negative attitudes you might have that you can restate in positive language? Identify five that relate to your job search and work. State them in both the negative and positive:

- Negative Attitude	**+ Positive Attitude**
1. _____	_____
_____	_____
_____	_____

2. _____   _____
   _____   _____
   _____   _____
   _____   _____

3. _____   _____
   _____   _____
   _____   _____
   _____   _____

4. _____   _____
   _____   _____
   _____   _____
   _____   _____

5. _____   _____
   _____   _____
   _____   _____

Resources for Changing Attitudes and Attracting Success

There's nothing better for exercising the mind and developing new attitudes than a good book shared with others. If you have difficulty reading, consider listening to audiobooks which are very popular these days and available in most libraries. If you don't read much, this would be a good time to develop a serious reading habit, especially focused on self-help books that encourage you to think outside the box as well as motivate you to take actions you might not otherwise take on your own. It's also a good way to share ideas with others who are preparing for re-entry. Perhaps you could form a re-entry book club where each member would report on a particular book. Develop some group-focused assignments related to a variety of important re-entry success questions, such as these:

- What useful things did I learn?
- How can I put the ideas into practice over the next 12 months?
- What additional information do I need to develop a sound re-entry plan?

You'll find numerous paper and electronic books, audiobooks, videos, and podcasts specializing in developing positive thinking and productive attitudes. Most are designed to transform the thinking and perceptions of individuals by changing negative attitudes. One of the major themes underlying these products is that you can change your life through positive thinking, new attitudes, and discovering the law of attraction. Individuals whose lives are troubled, for example, can literally transform themselves by changing their thinking in new and positive directions. Somewhat controversial and a form of pseudoscience, nonetheless, these products are especially popular with people in sales careers, such as real estate and insurance, who must constantly stay motivated, focused, and positive in the face of making cold calls that result in numerous rejections. Positive thinking helps them get through the day, the week, and the month despite numerous rejections that would normally dissuade most people from continuing to pursue more sales calls that result in even more rejections.

One of the most influential books on self-transformation through positive thinking is Napoleon Hill's ***Think and Grow Rich***. This single book has had a tremendous impact on the development of the positive thinking industry, which now includes hundreds of motivational speakers and gurus who produce numerous seminars, books, and audio programs for the true believers who think they can attract success through positive thoughts. Other popular books and authors include:

Keith Harrell	***Attitude is Everything***
Napoleon Hill and W. Clement Stone	***Success Through a Positive Mental Attitude***
Dr. Norman Vincent Peale	***The Power of Positive Thinking***
	Six Attitudes for Winners
Anthony Robbins	***Personal Power***
	Unlimited Power
	Awaken the Giant Within
	Live With Passion
	Money, Master the Game
Dr. Robert H. Schuller	***You Can Become the Person You Want to Be***
	The Be Happy Attitudes
Dale Carnegie	***How to Win Friends and Influence People***
Rhonda Byrne	***The Secret***
Les Brown	***Live Your Dream***
Joel Osteen	***Become a Better You***
	Your Best Life Now
David Schwartz	***The Magic of Thinking Big***
Zig Ziglar	***How to Get What You Want***
Og Mandino	***Secrets of Success***
Brian Tracy	***Change Your Thinking, Change Your Life***
	Create Your Own Future
	Eat That Frog!
	Focal Point
	Maximum Achievement

Steve Chandler	***100 Ways to Motivate Yourself***
	Reinventing Yourself
Bay and Macpherson	***Change Your Attitude***
Martin E.P. Seligman	***Learned Optimism***
Eckhart Tolle	***The Power of Now***
Carol S. Dweck	***Mindset: The New***
	Psychology of Success
Viktor E. Frankl	***Man's Search for Meaning***
Gary John Bishop	***Unfu*k Yourself***
Claude M. Bristol	***The Magic of Believing***
Wayne W. Dyer	***Excuses Begone!***

Many of these titles are in audiobook format.

As you will quickly discover, a positive attitude that focuses on the future is one of the most powerful motivators for achieving success. Any of these recommended books will get you started on the road to changing your attitudes as well as your life. They are filled with fascinating stories of self-transformation, motivational language, and exercises for developing positive attitudes for success.

For a powerful alternative to the popular pseudoscientific positive thinking and laws of attraction approaches, see Richard Bandler's ground-breaking neuro-linguistic programming approach:

> ***Get the Life You Want: The Secrets to Quick***
> ***and Lasting Change With Neuro-Linguistic Programming***

Here's an important life-changing tip: Get serious about shaping your future by committing yourself to reading or listening to at least one of these books over the next two weeks. Set aside at least one hour each day to read a book or listen to a program that can literally change your life. Such books and programs will both exercise your mind and inspire you to be your best!

5

Develop a Purpose in Your Life

"When you have a purpose in life, you live a meaningful life. You look forward to tomorrow because it's another important day in a very special life."

WHY IN THE WORLD ARE YOU here, especially if you're sitting in a concrete and steel cage trying to survive this crazy joint? Is there some special reason you were born and lived the life you've lived thus far? What is your purpose? Do you have an objective? Do you have a written set of short-, intermediate-, and long-term goals? What do you want to do with the rest of your life? Where do you want to be and what do you want to be doing 30 years from now? What do you want your obituary to say when you die? Did your life have purpose? Did you leave a positive legacy as someone who touched the lives of others who looked up to you? Or did you just drift through what was a prematurely short and meaningless life where no one really cared if you dropped off the face of the earth like human trash?

People who lose their freedom often have lots of dreams about freedom. Increasingly divorced from reality, their dreams become illusions. And many of these individuals don't know how to make those dreams come true. No amount of dreaming or positive thinking will make you successful. Indeed, you have a lot of hard work ahead of you. But despite your current circumstances, you should be able to make some wonderful dreams, grounded in reality, come true.

Live a Purpose-Driven Life

If you're a religious or spiritual person, you've probably learned that all of God's children are special, including yourself. You may believe that you're here on earth with a purpose or a **calling**. Fitting into a much larger scheme of things, you have a particular **destiny** that you may or may not understand at present but which you need to fulfill before you die. The higher power or powers you submit to have determined who you are and what you will be and do in the future. When you escape your selfish self and submit to those powers, you begin to achieve true understanding. A heavy burden may be lifted as you begin to understand the **real you** and see the future through different lens. You discover who you are and what you are destined to be and do. Your future becomes very clear, and you begin to lead a very **meaningful life**. Accordingly, you try to live a life that is focused on your **purpose**.

People who organize their lives around their purpose tend to live very rich and rewarding lives despite occasional failures and tragedies. They achieve an inner strength and personal power that propel them forward. They learn to stay **focused** on what's really important in life. Given their focus, everything else in their life seems to fall in place – family, job, housing, finances, etc. When they stumble or fall down, they pick themselves up quickly and continue on what is a clear and purposeful path. They may occasionally get angry and depressed, but they soon snap out of it and move ahead with their lives. They know that *"this too shall pass"* on their way to fulfilling their purpose.

> *People who organize their lives around their purpose tend to live very rich and rewarding lives despite failures and tragedies.*

While such people may not be materially rich, they have a wealth of wisdom and relationships that make life so rewarding. When they leave this earth, they leave an important **legacy** behind – they lived a purpose-driven life that had a positive impact on other people. They had a truly wonderful life.

Everyone has shortcomings and experiences disappointments, failures, and tragedies. No doubt about it – life can be tough even for those who are blessed with success. While you may occasionally fail and experience disappointments, nonetheless, you were basically created to do good. Even your present incarceration has a purpose in your life – perhaps this experience is an important step toward understanding your purpose and charting a life with greater meaning. Maybe it's **your moment** to alter your mindset to create the inner strength and personal power you need to pursue your purpose in life. Above all, this may be your moment to finally determine what you really want to do with your life and plan your future accordingly.

Even if you're not a religious person, you've probably wondered why you're here on earth. If you've ever been depressed, you know what it's like when you feel worthless and nothing really matters. Taking these feelings to an extreme, suicidal people feel so worthless that they decide to take the ultimate action – their life is not worth living.

If you learn only one thing from this book, it is this – **you need to identify your purpose and organize your life accordingly**. Once you identify your purpose, many things in your life will fall into place. Your attitude and motivation will change, and you'll put yourself on the road to achieving the true freedom we discussed in Chapter 3.

Richard Leider and David Shapiro put much of what I discuss here in perspective in their book *Claiming Your Place At the Fire: Living the Second Half of Your Life On Purpose*. Using the metaphor of fire for people entering a new stage in the lives, they note that claiming one's place at the fire is all about **living a life on purpose** – an intended or designed life. We claim our place at the fire by:

> *"...courageously reexamining and rediscovering who we are, where we belong, what we care about, and what our life's purpose is.*

> *We believe that the second half of life offers us unique opportunities for growing whole, not old. When we claim our place at the fire – by recalling our stories, refinding our place, renewing our calling, and reclaiming our purpose – we ultimately embrace the deepest expression of who we really are."*

When you discover your purpose in life, which you should state as a vision or mission statement and a set of concrete achievable goals, you will have made the first big step in charting a new path to success. As noted motivation guru Earl Nightingale observes,

> *"People with goals succeed because they know where they are going. It's as simple as that."*

I would add that the reverse of this simple notion of success is true:

> *"If you don't know where you're going and you're not in control, chances are you'll end up somewhere unintended, such as where you are today! That's not good."*

Not surprisingly, you'll probably meander joylessly through life doing *"a little of this and a little of that"* but nothing of any particular significance. While you may have some fun along the way and affect others, your life will lack meaning and you may ask the same question many other people without a purpose lament – *"Is this all there is to life?"*

If your life lacks purpose, you're not the captain of your ship. Indeed, your life may take the path of the rudderless and sinking boat on stormy waters – you're going nowhere but around and down. Such a life can be scary and painful as it spirals out of control and into depression, or worse.

With purpose and goals, you'll have direction in your life. You'll be able to specify your destinations and get there under your own power. While you may experience some rough waters along the way, at least you know where you are going and you're equipped to make a successful journey. Best of all, you'll be the captain of your own ship!

Let's explore a few ideas that will help you better formulate your mission statement, set goals, and develop an action plan for successful re-entry. Start by addressing these 12 questions:

1. What's really important in my life?

_____

_____

_____

2. Who do I care the most about in my life?

_____

_____

_____

3. What good things have I done with my life?

_____

_____

_____

_____

4. What are my three greatest strengths?

1. _____

2. _____

3. _____

5. Who has had the greatest impact on my life and why?

_____

_____

_____

6. What do I most enjoy doing?

_____

_____

_____

7. What is my ideal or dream job?

_____

_____

_____

8. What are some of my hidden talents few people know about?

_____

_____

_____

_____

9. If I could change three things about my life, what would they be?

1. _____

2. _____

3. _____

10. What things do I most admire in others?

_____

_____

_____

11. What five things would I like to do before I die?

    1. _____

    2. _____

    3. _____

    4. _____

    5. _____

12. What is my purpose in life?

_____

_____

_____

_____

Refer to your responses to these 12 questions when you start drafting your mission statement on pages 61-62. Your answers to these questions include the basic elements – values, accomplishments, dreams – for developing a powerful personal mission statement.

And Before You Die

If you have difficulty answering the above questions or want to generate more information for developing your mission statement, I recommend completing these two "obituary" exercises for identifying the things your would like to do or accomplish before you die. Take out three pieces of paper and write your obituary. First, make a list of things you want to do or accomplish in response to this lead-in statement: *"Before I die, I want to..."*

Before I die, I want to . . .

    1. _____

    2. _____

    3. _____

    4. _____

    5. _____

    6. _____

Second, write a newspaper article, which is actually your obituary for 10 years from now. Stress your accomplishments over the coming 10-year period.

My Obituary

Obituary for Mr./Ms. _____ to appear in the _____ Newspaper in the year 20_____.

_____

_____

_____

_____

_____

_____

_____

_____

_____

_____

_____

_____

_____

_____

_____

_____

Develop Your Mission Statement

A mission statement is a declaration of your purpose in life. Expressing your major values, it states who you are, what you stand for, and how you plan to live your life.

Major corporations, government agencies, and nonprofit organizations, including charities and churches, regularly develop mission statements that incorporate their values and organize their operations around key principles for achieving goals and measuring their performance. For example, the mission statement for the Ohio Department of Rehabilitation and Correction is this:

> *The Ohio Department of Rehabilitation and Correction protects and supports Ohioans by ensuring that adult felony offenders are effectively supervised in environments that are safe, humane, and appropriately secure. In partnership with communities, we will promote citizen safety and victim reparation. Through rehabilitative and restorative programming, we seek to instill in offenders an improved sense of responsibility and the capacity to become law-abiding members of society.*

Many individuals develop personal mission statements to guide their lives and careers. Some of the best such mission statements are short and to the point – one to two sentences. They also include timelines and measurable outcomes. After all, you want to be able to measure your progress toward achieving your mission or goals. If not, your mission statement may be very unrealistic. It should motivate you to achieve end results!

Keep in mind that a mission statement is not something that you just throw together in a few minutes. Important things in life take a great deal of time and thought. Indeed, you may struggle a lot in coming up with a simple but powerful 25- to 50-word mission statement. Don't be surprised if it takes hours, weeks, or even months to develop and refine a mission statement that is right for you. That's okay. The important thing is to get it right rather than to get it done quickly. Draft a basic statement and then move on and revise it over and over until you can look at it and say *"Aha! That's exactly what I want to do with my life."* It should reflect the **real you**, which also will become the **new you**.

Many mission statements focus on jobs and careers. Since you will spend much of your life working, and work gives meaning to life, you'll want to develop a **career mission statement**. These can be either self-centered or other-centered or incorporate both. Take, for example, the following career mission statements:

Self-centered career mission statements:

Become a successful landscape architect making $100,000 a year by age 35.

Own and operate a $6+ million a year landscape business by age 45.

Other-centered career mission statements:

Become an HIV/AIDS case worker in the city of Baltimore within three months after release, a position that would play an important role in saving lives and improving the quality of life in the city's many troubled neighborhoods.

Become director of a $5+ million community-based rehabilitation center in St. Louis within 10 years that will significantly lower the city's rate of drug and alcohol abuse.

More general but closely related **personal mission statements** might approximate the following:

Self-centered personal mission statements:

To find happiness, joy, love, and respect in my life by acquiring more education, a loving family, and a rewarding career by age 40.

Other-centered personal mission statements:

To make a difference in this world by providing leadership by age 40 in the field of drug and alcohol abuse. Develop innovative approaches to recovery involving special education programs and supportive employment environments.

Please note that each of these mission statements expresses **key values** and includes **measurable goals** and **dates**. In other words, they weren't statements of lofty goals that could not be measured. In fact, some people write themselves a time capsule check for the amount of money they say they will make by a particular date. If, for example, your goal is to have $1 million in the bank by the year 2027, write yourself a $1 million check dated for your birthday in 2027 and keep it in an important place (try your wallet) that will constantly remind you where you plan be financially in 2027. This exercise has helped many successful people keep focused on their financial goals and achieve them beyond their wildest dreams! If your goal is to become a leader in a particular field by the year 2027, you may want to give yourself a community leadership award and treat it similarly to the $1 million check. Write out an appreciation award for a specific date and put it in your wallet as a frequent reminder of where you plan to be in the year 2027 – at an awards dinner receiving your special award for your exceptional character and leadership.

Try to develop two different sets of mission statements that are both self-centered and other-centered. Make sure they incorporate these six key elements of good mission statement writing (You also can produce a free mission statement online by going to www.nightingale.com/personal-mission-statement):

1. Focuses on the **future**
2. Is **brief** but powerful
3. Expresses your key **values**
4. Includes a timeline or target **date**
5. Can be measured for **results** or outcomes
6. Focuses on a particular **audience**

Try to draft rough mission statements by following this basic format of **values – timeline – outcomes – audience**:

I want to _____ *by age* _____ *that will result*
                    things you want to achieve   number

in _____ *for* _____.
          measurable outcome   targeted audience

Now, re-state your mission statement in a format and language that approximates the examples I outlined on page 60:

My self-centered career mission statement:

_____

_____

_____

_____

_____

My other-centered career mission statement:

_____

_____

_____

_____

Can you now combine these two statements into a single mission statement that is both self- and other-centered?

_____

_____

_____

_____

Now, write yourself an **award** (a check, complimentary words appearing on a medal or plaque, a letter of appreciation, something that says you're special and/or exceptional) that you expect to receive on your birthday in 2027 for accomplishing the mission you outlined today.

```



```

Set Meaningful Goals

In my companion workbook, *The Ex-Offender's Quick Job Hunting Guide* (pages 46-76), I include extensive sections on how to identify your interests, assess your motivated abilities and skills (MAS), and develop a powerful objective related to your job and career interests. I highly recommend working through those sections in order to relate your mission statement to a career objective. If you do this, you will have completed the most important steps in developing a road map to your future. You will become the captain of your ship as you navigate some rough waters ahead. In the end, you will achieve true freedom because you will be doing exactly what you should be doing as you live a very purposeful life.

Develop a Realistic Re-Entry Plan

Your re-entry plan should focus on specific goals you want to accomplish that also are related to your mission statement. It's always best to identify goals that are linked to a calendar. In other words, you need to identify what it is you want to accomplish next week, next month, next year, and five, 10, 20, or 30 years from now. Start by identifying five things you plan to accomplish (outcomes) during the first 90 to 180 days after release. Try to be as specific as possible for the first four weeks – the most critical re-entry time period:

Week #1

1. _____
2. _____
3. _____
4. _____
5. _____

Week #2

1. _____
2. _____
3. _____
4. _____
5. _____

Week #3

1. _____
2. _____
3. _____
4. _____
5. _____

Week #4

1. _____
2. _____
3. _____
4. _____
5. _____

Month #2

    1. _____

    2. _____

    3. _____

    4. _____

    5. _____

Month #3

    1. _____

    2. _____

    3. _____

    4. _____

    5. _____

Month #4

    1. _____

    2. _____

    3. _____

    4. _____

    5. _____

Month #5

    1. _____

    2. _____

    3. _____

    4. _____

    5. _____

Month #6

    1. _____

    2. _____

    3. _____

    4. _____

    5. _____

If you're only able to identify accomplishments for the first week or two, you'll need to rethink what it is you need to do and whom you need to contact for those other critical weeks and months. Remember, most ex-offenders get themselves into trouble (violate parole, get re-arrested for a crime, etc.) during the first six months after release. The easy part of this planning process is filling in the blanks for the first two weeks. But after that, you're heading into potentially troubled waters if you don't have a realistic plan of action to succeed on the outside.

This is a good time to think real hard about what it is you want to do with the rest of your life and then commit yourself to taking the necessary actions to succeed on the outside. You can do this by writing out the specific things you need to do during the first six months. This will become your **road map** to successful re-entry. For a more extensive treatment of this subject, see the latest edition of my ***99 Days to Re-Entry Success Journal: Your Weekly Planning and Implementation Tool for Staying Out for Good!*** (Impact Publications).

Do an Annual Check-Up

Our focus on identifying your purpose and developing a re-entry plan related to that purpose is designed to put full wind in your sails for successfully re-entering the Free World. While it's important to initially identify your purpose – establish a baseline – your mission statement and goals should not be carved in stone. Neither should they be so flexible that they constantly change and thus become useless or meaningless for giving you direction in your life.

Unfortunately, the nature of prisons and jails is such that inmates become increasingly divorced from the realities of the outside world – the longer you remain incarcerated, the more illusions you acquire. Many inmates face this dilemma:

> *How can I develop a realistic objective for surviving in the outside world when my reality has been so perverted while trying to survive inside this institution?*

Once on the outside, you face many new realities that may affect the mission statement and goals you developed behind bars in preparation for release. In fact, it will take you two to five years of challenging adjustments before you make it on the outside for good.

I recommend that you do an annual mission check-up – review and refine your mission statement and related goals on your birthday, which also will become a "mission rebirth day." What has changed in your life since you last wrote that mission statement? What new experiences, interests, and relationships have expanded your view of the world? Is there a better way of stating your mission statement?

You should do a similar annual check-up concerning your job or career. Assuming you have a resume (see my companion ***Best Resumes and Letters for Ex-Offenders***), take it out and update it. Has your career objective

It will probably take two to five years of challenging adjustments before you make it on the outside for good.

changed? What new skills have you acquired? What new accomplishments can you add to your resume? Do you need more education and training? Who would be happy to serve as a reference concerning your work skills, accomplishments, and character?

As we noted earlier, everyone goes through seasons in life. Why not make a review of your mission statement, goals, and resume an annual event? If you do this, you'll be able to better shape and control your seasons in life.

Recommended Resources on Purposeful Living

The following resources should help you better understand and develop your own mission statement, goals, and plans for the future. Most are books which can be found in libraries. Similar to the resources at the end of Chapter 4, most of them also can be found online at www.impactpublications.com.

- *7 Habits of Highly Effective People*
- *Become a Better You*
- *Choices That Change Lives: 15 Ways to Find More Purpose, Meaning, and Joy*
- *Claiming Your Place at the Fire*
- *How to Find Your Mission in Life*
- *I Will Not Die an Unlived Life: Reclaiming Purpose and Passion*
- *Life is in the Transitions: Mastering Change at Any Age*
- *Life Reimagined: Discovering Your New Life Possibilities*
- *A Life You Were Born to Live: A Guide to Finding Your Life Purpose*
- *Live Your Calling: A Practical Guide to Finding and Fulfilling Your Mission in Life*
- *Man's Search for Meaning*
- *The Monk Who Sold His Ferrari: A Fable About Fulfilling Your Dreams and Reaching Your Destiny*
- *A New Earth: Awakening to Your Life's Purpose*
- *Perfecting Your Purpose: 40 Days to a More Meaningful Life*
- *Plato and Platypus Walk Into a Bar*
- *The Power of Intention: Learning to Co-create Your World Your Way*
- *The Power of Purpose: Creating Meaning in Your Life and World*
- *The Promise: God's Purpose and Plan for When Life Hurts*
- *The Purpose-Driven Life*
- *Re-Imagining Life on the Outside*
- *Repacking Your Bags*
- *The Rhythm of Life: Living Every Day With Passion and Purpose*
- *Success is Not an Accident: Change Your Choices, Change Your Life*
- *Think Like a Monk: Train Your Mind for Peace and Purpose*
- *Work Reimagined: Uncover Your Calling*
- *Your Life Calling: Reimagining the Rest of Your Life*

If you have access to the Internet, I recommend visiting these useful websites for developing your mission statement:

- articles.bplans.com/writing-a-mission-statement
- www.missionstatements.com
- www.zety.com/blog/personal-mission-statement
- www.high5test.com/personal-mission-statement

Don't Cheat Yourself!

In the end, you may find the information and exercises in this chapter to be the most life-altering of any presented in this workbook. Just make sure you work through this chapter in as deliberate manner as possible. If you just skip over this material, or only spend a few minutes trying to quickly fill in the blanks because it was "assigned" to you by an instructor, you're literally cheating yourself from achieving the true freedom I discussed in Chapter 3.

> *Cut the life-shortening crap and learn to grow old, happy, and wise – and live with passion!*

Do yourself and your loved ones a favor – produce a mission statement that has the potential of transforming your life in the years ahead. Discover what a really meaningful life centered on purpose can be. Cut the life-shortening crap and learn to grow old, happy, and wise – and live with passion! With the help of the questions and exercises in this chapter, you should be able to experience your own "Aha!" moment. Once you do, your path to the future will become very clear, and you'll know what you need to do to achieve re-entry success. Only **you** can do it!

> *"It's really not all that complicated:*
> *The purpose of life is to live a life on purpose."*

6

Get Smart Through Education, Training, and Lifelong Learning

"Success in the outside world is all about education, training, and lifelong learning. If you'll get smart and stay smart, chances are you'll stay out for good!"

I F YOU DROPPED OUT OF SCHOOL or have gone through life with a learning disability, such as dyslexia or attention deficit disorder (ADD or ADHD), you've got some serious strikes against you in a society that highly values education, training, and lifelong learning. In fact, studies show that the majority of inmates lack a high school diploma and nearly 70 percent have reading problems when they enter jail or prison. Not surprisingly, many ex-offenders lack the necessary skills to function in today's increasingly demanding job market as well as basic life skills for functioning in society.

The good news is that many inmates take advantage of education programs. Many earn a GED and/or college credits and acquire vocational and technical training while incarcerated. That's great because here's what employers want – a smart and skilled workforce!

We also know that **education is the great escalator** in society. Indeed, there's a strong relationship between education, employment, and income – the higher your education, the higher your income and employability. See the latest statistics from the U.S. Department of Labor on page 69.

It's this simple – get more education and you'll probably make more money and live a happier and more secure life. Stay uneducated and you're in trouble!

Prepare for a New Learning World

Employers today need highly skilled individuals who have basic workplace skills as well as demonstrate the capacity to listen, learn, and excel in their work. For them, education is not something that ends in school or is demonstrated on a piece of paper called a diploma, certificate, or degree.

Earnings and Unemployment Rates
by educational attainment, 2021

Unemployment rate in 2014 (percent)	Education attained	Median weekly earnings in 2014
1.5	Doctoral degree	$1,909
1.8	Professional degree	$1,924
2.6	Master's degree	$1,574
3.5	Bachelor's degree	$1,334
4.6	Associate degree	$963
5.5	Some college, no degree	$899
6.2	High school diploma	$809
8.3	Less than high school diploma	$626

Today education means continuous on-the-job training and lifelong learning. Given the rapid changes in today's technology and its application to the workplace, individuals need to be willing and able to acquire new skills. At the very least, you need to be able to read, comprehend, follow instructions, and communicate well. Most important of all, you need to demonstrate that learning is something you **value** and welcome in your life. If you equate learning with something you hate – school – it's time to disabuse yourself of that falsehood. Learning is something you need to enthusiastically welcome in your life. Learning is to the mind what physical exercise is to the body – a form of fitness you must constantly engage in if you want to stay healthy and perhaps get wealthy and wise in the process!

Many ex-offenders who re-enter the Free World discover they also need to brush up on their **life skills**, from handling money to playing music, using a cell phone, operating a computer, and driving a car. If you've been locked up behind a fire wall for more than two years, chances are some critical elements in the outside world may have passed you by, especially anything related to computers and the Internet. In fact, you may go through culture shock as you encounter both the familiar and unfamiliar in the outside world, starting with automatic flush toilets and touch-free sinks and hand-drying machines in public restrooms!

Learning is to the mind what exercise is to the body – a form of fitness you must constantly engage in if you want to stay healthy.

For example, more and more people now use ATMs and do online banking rather than go to a teller window at a bank to deposit and withdraw money. Many stores (especially grocery and home building supply stores) now operate self-checkout lanes that require you to follow computerized instructions for entering, bagging, and paying for your purchases. Many companies require applicants to apply for jobs online rather than use computer kiosk or submit paper resumes and applications. You need basic computer literacy skills in order to function in this challenging new digital world.

If you learned to program and operate a VCR or DVD machine before you were incarcerated, you'll now find that VCRs and DVD players have gone the way of the buggy whip and typewriter – obsolete and discarded. Even desktop and laptop computers are increasingly being replaced by powerful hand-held devices. You'll be entering a world where you'll increasingly download files to new generation of smart phones with 5G technology and apps.

Today's newest computers have highly sophisticated operating systems and advanced software that require users to follow complicated directions and acquire online help for solving problems. Apple's new generation of Macs come complete with software for managing photos (iPhoto), making movies (iMovie), composing music (Garage Band), and downloading and playing audio and movies (iTunes) – truly creative entertainment centers that also appeal to professionals who work with sophisticated graphics and audio. From smart phones to smart watches and laptop computers, many Apple devices can now be synced to one another, with data backed up in "the cloud" (Internet-based servers) rather than on your computer's hard drive. Software programs are increasingly being replaced by thousands of applications (apps).

More and more cars are highly computerized as well as include sophisticated voice-activated navigation systems. Even your basic television is now a complicated entertainment center tied to costly monthly cable and/or satellite fees.

The Internet continues to expand rapidly, with online shopping becoming as normal as getting in a car and going to the store. However, if you don't own a credit card or if you are unbanked, chances are you won't be able to shop online.

There's a lot to learn and re-learn once you get out into the Free World. Much of this learning requires the ability to read, comprehend, follow directions, and use a telephone, computer, and the Internet to get help. People without basic reading, comprehension, and learning skills as well as a digital-receptive mind find this new world to be extremely frustrating. Indeed, many people lacking new technology-driven life skills simply don't fit into the new high-tech world.

Become a Learning Machine

If you lack a high school diploma and failed to take advantage of opportunities to get your GED while incarcerated, what can I say? Not only was that short-sighted on your part, but where is your head? To begin with, and despite your excuses (I've heard them all), you made a bad choice by not getting your high school diploma. And now you continue to demonstrate your inability to make good choices.

The very least you can do for yourself is to get a GED. It will serve you well in the years ahead. It's an investment in yourself. You'll feel good when you get it! It's something you can include on your resume as well as mention on job applications and include as part of your "story" about what you have done to improve yourself while incarcerated.

Employers expect applicants to have at a very minimum a high school diploma or GED. If you don't have these credentials, you raise a big red flag about your level of literacy, choices, motivations, and capabilities to do good work. Can you read, write, speak properly, and calculate? Why did you drop out? Are you a quitter? Why should I hire someone who didn't even complete high school or get a GED? What other negative things will I learn about this person?

The same can be said for acquiring vocational and technical skills. Hopefully, you've taken advantage of educational programs while incarcerated. If not, you'll need to develop a good story about why you passed up such opportunities for self-improvement.

Whether you are incarcerated or on the outside, you should regularly participate in education and training programs for five main reasons:

1. Acquire useful knowledge and skills for work and life.
2. Exercise, strengthen, and focus your mind.
3. Enhance your resume and job applications.
4. Add substance to your story of transformation.
5. Give yourself more freedom and control.

Best of all, acquiring education and applying it to your life and work will enhance your **self-esteem**. Education is something no one can ever take away from you.

Regardless of decisions you've made in the past, it's never too late to acquire education and training. Many high schools and community colleges offer adult education programs. One of the very first things you should do upon release is to participate in an education program that will help improve your skills. If you know where you are going upon release, you should get information on local adult education programs. You can get such information through parole/probation officers, YMCAs or YWCAs, high schools, community colleges, libraries, churches, and community-based organizations that assist ex-offenders with re-entry.

Once you get a job, be sure to check with your employer about on-the-job education and training programs. Not only will you impress the employer with your interest in acquiring more education and training, but you also will better position yourself for promotions and advancements. Take, for example, one of America's best employers – Costco. From top to bottom, this company is committed to education and training. Indeed, 80 percent of management's job is to teach their employees to become the very best in the business. One way of doing this is through Costco University, which is an online learning center with virtual classrooms, e-learning courses, certifications, and training manuals. Each department within Costco develops its own curriculum using internal subject matter experts or outside consultants. One thing Costco employees know for sure is that they are expected to constantly learn in what is a very dynamic and exciting work environment. They participate in a **culture of learning**. The end result is one of America's top-performing companies and a great place to work.

People With Learning Disabilities

Unfortunately, many ex-offenders have had bad learning experiences, such as feeling stupid or being made fun of by others for doing poorly in the classroom. Experiencing failure and possessing low self-esteem, many such people get angry, express disdain for learning, drop out of school, and join the wrong crowd.

Fortunately, educators are increasingly aware of why some people don't learn like others and why many students fail and drop out of school. One reason is that people respond to different **learning styles**. Indeed, traditional classroom learning – sit still, listen, wait your turn, be polite, don't disrupt, participate in group activities – is not for everyone. Some people learn best on their on, in chaotic settings, with a tutor or mentor, or interactively online. In other words, many ex-offenders who have low education achievement may respond better to nontraditional learning styles.

Many children with learning problems have been misdiagnosed as slow learners and mentally deficient when in fact they suffer from one of two major learning disabilities – dyslexia and attention deficit disorder (ADD). **Dyslexia** especially explains a lot of reading problems – Johnny doesn't read because the letters in words don't appear in the same order as they are written and thus Johnny has difficulty pronouncing words and comprehending sentences and paragraphs. He has never read a book and can't understand why some people love reading books. Johnny gets very frustrated trying to read. In fact, he doesn't read because he's dyslexic. But other people often think he's stupid. As a result, Johnny has low self-esteem and gets very frustrated and angry. He may drop out of school because he doesn't do well, kids make fun of him, teachers criticize him or simply give up by sticking him in a special classroom of "slow learners" who also seem to be disproportionately made up of troublemakers. Indeed, we know a disproportionate number of ex-offenders are dyslexic and/or have attention deficit disorder. In fact, maybe up to 50 percent of your fellow inmates experience these learning disabilities!

Many people with dyslexia are known to be very creative and successful. These famous people in entertainment, arts, sports, politics, and business are dyslexic:

- Ansel Adams
- Mohammad Ali
- Harry Belafonte
- Richard Branson
- Cher
- Agatha Christie
- Sir Winston Churchill
- Tom Cruise
- Leonardo da Vinci
- Walt Disney
- Thomas Edison
- Henry Ford
- Danny Glover
- Whoopi Goldberg
- Tommy Hilfiger
- Thomas Jefferson
- Magic Johnson
- John Lennon
- Jay Leno
- General George Patton
- Pablo Picasso
- Keanu Reeves
- John D. Rockefeller
- Charles Schwab
- Steven Spielberg
- Ted Turner
- George Washington
- Woodrow Wilson

A widespread problem, dyslexia is now very treatable since it was discovered to be a learning disability. If you feel you might have the symptoms of dyslexia – have difficulty reading, letters in words get reversed, get easily frustrated with reading materials, hate having to read out loud in front of others – you are well advised to seek assistance. You may quickly discover that you have a learning disability that can be corrected.

Once you are treated, a whole new world of learning may open to you. In fact, you may redirect your anger to the very problem – dyslexia – that has for so long gone undiagnosed and possibly contributed to your current situation.

Attention deficit disorder (ADD) is another widespread learning problem that discourages individuals from learning. Individuals with ADD have difficulty concentrating for very long. Their minds wander a lot. They may start reading or begin a project but after two minutes their minds are elsewhere. As a result, they can't keep focused on what they are supposed to be doing. They may have difficulty completing tasks. As students in school, their work is often incomplete and they may have difficulty following instructions.

Some individuals with ADD also may suffer from ADHD – Attention Deficit Hyperactivity Disorder. In these cases, their lack of attention is complicated by hyperactivity, which is often gets translated into disruptive behavior. The classic signs that young people have ADHD include **poor concentration** and **impulsiveness**. They are **easily distracted** and **hyperactive**.

While ADD and ADHD are most pronounced in children, adults also are known to have ADD and ADHD. When such people become older, ADD and ADHD can negatively affect their work and relationships. They may manifest their ADHD in these behaviors: inattentive, impatient, and impulsive. When looking for a job, they may have difficulty with job interviews, because they fail to make a good first impression – their inattentiveness may be interpreted as a lack of respect for the interviewer and a lack of interest in the job. They may not listen well and thus interrupt the interviewer. They also are known to talk quickly and speak loudly or do just the opposite – say little and speak softly. Once on the job, they may appear disorganized and careless because they have many unfinished projects, incomplete ideas, and a cluttered workplace – behaviors they replicate at home.

Not surprisingly, if left undiagnosed, adults with ADD or ADHD may have difficulty both getting and keeping a job. Similar to dyslexia, ADD and ADHD can be treated, which is usually in the form of therapy and drugs (usually Ritalin).

Many very famous and extremely successful people have been known to have ADD or ADHD. You should recognize some of these names:

- Albert Einstein
- Beethoven
- Alexander Graham Bell
- President George Bush (both 41 and 43)
- Andrew Carnegie
- Christopher Columbus
- Tom Cruise
- Leonardo da Vinci
- Bill Gates
- Ernest Hemingway
- Dustin Hoffman
- Howard Hughes
- Thomas Jefferson
- Magic Johnson
- Michael Jordan
- John F. Kennedy
- Robert Kennedy
- Evel Knievel
- John Lennon
- Abraham Lincoln
- Mozart
- Napoleon
- Jack Nicholson
- General George Patton
- Pablo Picasso
- H. Ross Perot

- Elvis Presley
- Joan Rivers
- John D. Rockefeller
- Pete Rose
- Steven Spielberg
- Sylvester Stallone
- Ted Turner
- Robin Williams

Some of these famous people also had dyslexia. If you have this problem, you'll in good company! But you first need to know that you have this treatable problem before you can move ahead and become a learning machine.

Identify Your Education Needs

Respond to the following questions with as much information as possible. There are no right or wrong answers to these questions.

1. What is your education and training background?

Schools attended	Degree/Certificate	Dates
_____	_____	_____
_____	_____	_____
_____	_____	_____
_____	_____	_____
_____	_____	_____
_____	_____	_____

Your usual grade performance (mark where you fit on the grade line):

```
|—————————————————————————————————————|
   A        B        C        D        F
```

Subjects you most enjoyed:

1. _____
2. _____
3. _____
4. _____
5. _____

Best skills you acquired:

_____

_____

_____

Equipment you learned to use:

_____

_____

Special educational accomplishments and/or honors:

_____

_____

_____

What you most liked about your educational experiences:

_____

_____

_____

What you least liked about your educational experiences:

_____

_____

_____

Teacher you most admired. Why?

_____

_____

_____

2. **If someone gave you $50,000 that could only be used for purchasing education and training services, how would you spend that money?**

_____

_____

_____

_____

3. **If no one gave you money for education and training services, what would you do to improve your knowledge and skills?**

_____

_____

_____

_____

4. What do you see as your major educational needs in the next 10 years?

_____

_____

_____

_____

_____

Test for Learning Disabilities

Complete the following exercise – check the appropriate boxes on the right – to determine if you might have one of the learning disabilities we discussed earlier in this chapter.

	Yes	No
1. I got poor grades in school.	❑	❑
2. I dropped out of school.	❑	❑
3. I used to get into trouble in school.	❑	❑
4. I have difficulty reading.	❑	❑
5. I don't like to read out loud.	❑	❑
6. I avoid reading books.	❑	❑
7. I sometimes act impulsively – do things without thinking.	❑	❑
8. I have a hard time sitting still for long.	❑	❑
9. My mind often wanders.	❑	❑
10. I have difficulty concentrating.	❑	❑
11. I'm easily distracted.	❑	❑
12. I often don't complete projects.	❑	❑
13. I don't learn well in traditional classrooms.	❑	❑
TOTALS	_____	_____

If you checked "Yes" to more than five of these statements, you may be dyslexic or have ADD or ADHD. You need to talk to someone about what you need to do to improve your learning capabilities (drugs are probably out of the question if you are currently incarcerated). If you don't, you're likely to find yourself working in low-paying jobs without a future, frustrated and angry at trying to learn new things, and getting fired for impulsiveness, disorganization, and incompetence. This would be a tragedy when, in fact, you could have done something about your disability. Try to get help NOW!

Recommended Resources

Whatever you do, make sure you are fully using the educational and training resources available through your institution. Start by hanging out in the library and learning what's available through the education department. Similar to the resources recommended at the end of Chapters 4 and 5, most of the books mentioned in this section also can be found through www.impactpublications.com. Many correctional institutions offer GED programs and vocational and technical training programs.

If you think you have a learning disability, check with your institution's education department and the psychologist to see if you can be tested and treated. If you exhibit a great deal of hyperactivity and impulsive behavior, it may be that you have more than just a learning disability – some inmates are bipolar (also known as "manic depressive") because of their frequent mood swings. Accordingly, they exhibit hyper highs and depressing lows. This mental health issue, too, is treatable through drugs and therapy. Again, don't expect your institution to dispense drugs to inmates unless they exhibit serious mental illness, such as schizophrenia.

Check to see if your library has any of these books to help you better understand learning disabilities and mental health:

- *ADD/ADHD Checklist*
- *Complete Learning Disabilities Handbook*
- *Delivered From Distraction*
- *Dr. Bob's Guide to Stop ADHD in 18 Days*
- *Driven to Distraction*
- *The Gift of Dyslexia*
- *Learning Outside the Lines*
- *New Hope for People With Bipolar Disorder*
- *Overcoming Dyslexia*
- *Surviving Manic Depression*
- *Taking Charge of ADHD*
- *You Mean I'm Not Lazy, Stupid, or Crazy?*

If you don't have a high school diploma and wish to prepare for the GED, look for these GED preparation books as well as any courses available through your institution:

- *Barron's How to Prepare for the GED Test*
- *Cracking the GED*
- *GED Basics*
- *GED for Dummies*
- *Kaplan GED Test Prep Plus*
- *Master the GED*
- *McGraw-Hill's Preparation for the GED with CD-ROM*

Your institution may also have these GED preparation programs, which include a set of 29 DVDs for various state administered GEDs:

- *GED Review Series*
- *HISET Review Series*
- *TASC Review Series*

If you want to improve your basic literacy skills – reading, comprehension, grammar, spelling, math, vocabulary, writing, logic, and reading – I recommend checking out these useful books:

- *501 Grammar and Writing Questions*
- *501 Critical Reading Questions*
- *1001 Algebra Problems*
- *Grammar Success*
- *Practical Math Success*
- *Practical Spelling*
- *Practical Vocabulary*
- *Reading Comprehension Success*
- *Reasoning Skills Success*
- *Research and Writing Skills Success*
- *Vocabulary and Spelling Success*
- *Writing Skills Success*

Your institution may also have these popular multi-DVD training programs available for reference:

- *English Grammar*
- *Upgrade Your Communication Skills at Work*
- *Upgrade Your Reading Comprehension*
- *Upgrade Your Writing*

All of these books and DVD programs represent important skills employers expect from you in order to function effectively in their workplace.

If you're planning to go on to college, your library may also have some of these useful books on higher education:

- *10 Things Employers Want You to Learn in College*
- *Book of Majors*
- *College Majors and Careers*
- *Barron's Profiles of American Colleges*
- *Fiske Guide to Colleges*
- *Peterson's Four-Year Colleges*
- *Peterson's Two-Year Colleges*

7

Tell the Truth About the New You

---

*"While we all have stories to tell about ourselves,
the ex-offender's story should focus on what's most important
to the outside world – your self-transformation."*

WHO EXACTLY ARE YOU, especially after being locked in a cage for so long? Tell me about yourself. I really don't want to hear about your rap sheet, which I'm sure is both interesting and potentially scary. That's the past. I deal with the future – the new you. I don't want to know about where you were born or sad stories about your mother, father, sisters, or brothers. I'm vaguely interested in your weird body art – what possessed you to engage in such expressive behavior? Do you have some unresolved power, control, and/or self-esteem issues?

What I really want to know is what you have done with your life – your education, accomplishments, and especially your **patterns of behavior**. I want to know about your **most recent choices**, which are reflected in your character and habits – those things I'll have to live with if I decide to associate with you. Are you truthful, trustworthy, ethical, focused, and competent? What is your purpose? What have you done to permanently change your life? Is there really a new you or just delusional talk? Why should I work with you?

So tell me your story – I want to know the truth about the new you!

It's Truth Telling Time

You've been there before – telling your story. You've sliced and diced it. Perhaps you just made up an interesting story. That's called the art of lying. Maybe you took creative license and conveniently left out your rap sheet and a few time gaps while you were on the "inside." That's also a form of lying, which may be reflected on your resume.

And maybe now you're thinking about what to say when an employer asks you this knee-bending question – *"Have you ever been convicted of a crime?"* How you plan to answer that question says a lot about your character and where you are going with your life.

Will you tell the truth? The whole truth? Or just a little bit of the truth? Are you a truthful and trustworthy person or just another ex-con who engages in the art of conning?

As many ex-offenders who have gone through the re-entry process will tell you, telling the truth will indeed set you free. When you don't tell the truth, you're still in prison. Only after you've come completely clean by telling the truth about yourself will you be psychologically free. Whatever you do, don't keep yourself locked into a cage of lies.

In this chapter I want to examine how you can best tell the truth as you re-enter the Free World, a world that is not particularly friendly to ex-offenders, who are known to be less than truthful and trustworthy when it comes time to tell their story on application forms and resumes and during job interviews. After all, the majority end up back in jail.

There's Nowhere to Hide These Days

When you feel down, remember this important principle of life: **This, too, shall pass**. Give yourself time and your best effort. Your past will quickly pass if you are truthful.

Commit yourself to the truth – no more lies, cover-ups, or excuses to yourself or to others. If you can't tell the truth, then don't expect to get a job or keep a job for very long. Don't expect well-meaning people to maintain relations with you when you abuse them. This is especially true for jobs, employers, and companies with a future – those offering higher wages and greater responsibilities that lead to a long-term career.

Americans strongly believe in come-backs, fresh starts, and second acts – that you can be anything you want to be if only you will work hard at being the person you want to be.

If you think you can hide your record from employers, think again. You're a person with both a paper and electronic trail. Once you get your documents – birth certificate, driver's license, Social Security number, or state ID – you're real easy to find in systems employers regularly access when doing background checks. In today's increasingly high-tech, database-driven, and security-conscious society, there is no place to hide. Employers can easily and inexpensively access your employment, criminal, and credit records through a variety of electronic databases they routinely consult when doing background checks.

And if by chance you fool an unsuspecting employer about your background, odds are your criminal record will eventually catch up with you on the job. Your P.O. may check on you by calling your employer; an old prison buddy may unexpectedly show up; or someone you secretly told about your record may talk too much. Word gets around. When you come up for a promotion or make a job change involving a background check, your criminal record will probably resurface. When it does, your lie will be exposed and you'll be fired or passed over. Everything you worked for now changes for the worse because of your **failure to disclose**.

Rather than try to live a lie, **tell the truth in a positive way** – that you were incarcerated but changed your life by participating in educational, vocational, substance abuse, or anger control programs. Much of our society is into redemption and transformation – it forgives those who make sincere efforts to change their lives and tell the truth. When you tell the truth, you're not expected to go into all the details, but at least tell the truth that matters most to employers – that **you're not a risky hire**.

We all at times stumble and fall. It's how we pick ourselves up and move on with our lives that really counts. We especially admire people who overcome adversity. We strongly believe in comebacks, fresh starts, and second acts – that you can be anything you want to be if only you will work hard at being the person you want to be. We don't like being deceived and disappointed.

What Employers Want From You

It's not surprising what employers want from their employees – **truthfulness, character, and value**. They want to better **predict your future behavior** based upon a clear understanding of your past patterns of behavior. You can help them achieve this understanding by organizing your story around the qualities of truthfulness, character, and value – those exuding the 45 positive characteristics summarized on page 49.

> *Employers want* **truthfulness**, **character**, *and* **value** *– no lies, no scamming, no cheating.*

Employers try to hire individuals who are competent, intelligent, honest, enthusiastic, and likable. At the same time, many employers are suspicious of candidates, because they have encountered manipulators, scammers, and deceivers among job applicants. They actually hired some people who turned out to be the wrong choice for the job, costing the company money, embarrassing the hiring manager, and even endangering other employees in the workplace.

In fact, surveys indicate that nearly two-thirds of job seekers include inaccurate information on applications and resumes, from fictitious degrees, schools, and accomplishments to nonexisting employers, employment dates, positions, responsibilities, and awards. Some of these inaccuracies are unintentional, but others are deliberate lies in order to cover up not-so-hot backgrounds and to get the job. Many of these inaccuracies surface during job interviews as candidates give deceptive answers to questions, or during the first 90 days on the job when an employer has the chance to observe actual on-the-job behavior.

Employers aren't stupid, although some are naive. Dealing with people they really don't know well – basically strangers – they are suspicious about putting such people on the company payroll. If you assume you can manipulate employers, think again. Get over your misplaced sense of power and control, which indicates you may be headed for trouble in both the job market and the workplace.

Employers anticipate all types of personalities, motivations, and behaviors – positive, negative, and manipulative – from strangers who want a job. Books such as *Don't Hire a Crook*, *101 Mistakes Employers Make and How to Avoid Them*, *Hiring the Best*, *Hiring Smart*, and *The Safe Hiring Manual: The Complete Guide to Keeping*

Criminals, Imposters, and Terrorists Out of Your Workplace are on the reading lists of many employers. In fact, employers can tell you lots of stories about the characters they have met, hired, and fired!

While employers may appear to trust what you say, they also want to verify your credentials and observe what you actually do. This means conducting background and reference checks (over 95 percent of employers do this), asking probing behavior-based questions, subjecting candidates to multiple job interviews, and administering a variety of revealing tests (aptitude, drug, personality, psychological, and polygraph) to discover the truth about you. **Verification and observation** are the real basis for trust – not questionable resumes and clever conversations with strangers.

Above all, employers want **value** for their money – people who can do the job well. Take, for example, a survey by the National Association of Colleges and Employers. It found that college graduates with **strong communication skills and integrity** have a distinct advantage in the job market. The most highly valued candidates were ones who demonstrated strong communication skills, honesty/integrity, interpersonal/teamwork skills, and a strong work ethic. These skills were more highly valued than computer, leadership, and organizational skills. These tend to be the same skills employers look for in candidates who do not have a college degree. As an ex-offender, you need to make sure these highly desired skills are part of your skill set and clearly communicate them to employers.

At this stage in your job search, it's extremely important that you take a complete inventory of your skills so you can better communicate with employers what it is you do well and enjoy doing. Once you do this and formulate a clear objective, you will be on the road to finding the right job for you. Your self-assessment will end much of your confusion as you begin charting an exciting path to renewed job and life success. I outline how you can do this in these two companion volumes: *The Ex-Offender's Quick Job Hunting Guide* and *The Ex-Offender's New Job Finding and Survival Guide*.

Telling the Stupid Versus the Smart Truth

But how do you tell the truth when your story appears to be troubling to others? I make a clear distinction between being honest and being stupid. In the name of truthfulness and honesty, some people say the stupidest things about themselves. Focusing on their total history, they confess all their sins in excruciating and depressing detail. That's a good way to put some real distance between you and the person who is listening to your story!

When you tell your story, you should emphasize two things:

1. Your positives or strengths – those things you do well and enjoy doing.
2. What you've done to change your life for the better – things that assure the listener that you have a predictable pattern of behavior.

If, for example, you are asked about your conviction, don't focus on all the negative details about what you did, how you were caught and convicted, and all the bad things and people you experienced in prison. That would be stupid, and you would probably appear to be a beggar – *"Please help me; I've fallen and I can't get up!"* Instead, briefly mention that you were convicted of a crime (*"Yes, I was convicted of a drug offense"*) and immediately move on to what the listener really wants to know – what you've done to improve yourself since those fateful conviction and incarceration days and never again get into trouble. That listener wants to know about your **pattern of behavior** that may affect him, her, and others they work with. Take, for example, this "story" about being convicted:

> *"In many respects, going to jail was the best thing to happen to me. I was young and stupid when I messed up my life with drugs. It hurt me most when my mother died while I was locked up. She needed me, but I was doing prison time instead. I'm sure she forgave me, but her death was a life-changing event. Indeed, I decided to change my life. Since then, I've learned many lessons in life, including the importance of taking responsibility and having goals. I finished my GED, worked in the prison library, and took three college-level courses. I eventually want to complete a degree in computer science. I'm, of course, asking you to take a chance with me. I won't disappoint you. I know what I want to do and the life I want to live. I just ask that you understand where I'm going – not where I'm coming from."*

This truthful story emphasizes self-transformation – taking responsibility and initiative, acquiring marketable skills, and having goals or a purpose in life. This is the type of **smart truth** you need to be telling on the outside – not the stupid truth about all your sins. This truth focuses on the future rather than dwells on the past. The stupid truth should be between you, your God, and your parole/probation officer!

Formulate Your Truthful Story

As you complete the following exercises, be sure to refer to this discussion about the difference between the stupid truth and the smart truth. However, if you've done little or nothing to demonstrate a compelling smart truth, you've got a problem in telling an appealing story. You may want to re-assess what you've been doing with your life and start thinking in terms of self-transformation. Go back to Chapter 5 on living a life on purpose. It will help! Then return to this page and complete these exercises when you get your new act together.

1. Five important lessons I've learned in life:

1. _____

2. _____

3. _____

4. _____

5. _____

2. Negative things I don't need to tell about myself:

    1. _____

    2. _____

    3. _____

    4. _____

    5. _____

3. Positive things I should tell about myself:

    1. _____

    2. _____

    3. _____

    4. _____

    5. _____

4. Things I have done within the past five years to change my life for the better:

    1. _____

    2. _____

    3. _____

    4. _____

    5. _____

5. If someone on the outside asks you to *"Tell me about yourself,"* what would you say? Write out your "story" in the space below. Keep your story brief but very focused on what's important to the conversation. This story should take no more than three minutes to tell.

My "New You" Story

_____

_____

_____

_____

_____

8

Take Responsibility and Build Trust

*"Responsibility and trust go hand in hand. People of character
step up to the plate and take responsibility for their actions.
They develop strong bonds of trust – the superglue of relationships –
that serve them well throughout their life."*

P UT YOURSELF IN THE SHOES of people on the outside who only know you as an ex-offender or ex-con. You've done your time. So what do they have against you? What's their greatest fear? Why are they reluctant to hire you, live next door to you, extend you credit, or entrust their children or other valuables to your care? Is it your looks, something you said, or something you did that turned them off? What do you have to do to become an accepted member of the community?

The answer to these questions is very simple – it's all about being **Responsible And Trustworthy (RAT)**. If this is not part of your character, you better soon become a RAT person or you'll probably be back in another cage trying to figure out what went so wrong with your last attempt at re-entry success!

Always remember that America is an exceptionally **forgiving** society. It's willing to help those who have fallen, admit their mistakes, seek redemption, and take initiative. But it doesn't forget criminal behavior, especially among those who remain unrepentant and at risk of becoming repeat offenders. They particularly prize RAT people!

Take Responsibility and Ask Forgiveness

If you've not done so yet, you need to take responsibility for your actions. This cuts two ways. First, you need to come to terms with your past. You do this by taking responsibility for your behavior. It's a very simple issue – you've been doing time because you did the crime. Therefore, it's time to suck it in. Admit what you did was based on some bad choices you made, seek forgiveness (sincerely say you're sorry), and move on to the next stage of your life. If you're religious, you do this by confessing your sins and seeking forgiveness from a higher power rather than from your victims or family members, although you also need to speak truth to those you hurt.

If you're still in denial, blaming others, and feeling angry about your predicament, you'll never be able to move on to where you should be going. Your denial, blame, and anger will eat at you like a cancer, destroying your motivation and drive to succeed. Indeed, anger is just another form of **addiction** that is **self-destructive**. The best way to free yourself is to let go of your anger by admitting responsibility and seeking forgiveness.

> *Anger is just another form of addiction that is self-destructive."*

Admit it and move on. If you don't, you'll remain stuck in a rut that will most likely lead back to where you are at present. Start by completing these exercises on responsibility and forgiveness:

1. **Take responsibility by admitting what you did that got you where you are today:**

My Admission of Responsibility

_____

_____

_____

_____

_____

_____

_____

2. **Write forgiveness letters to the major audiences that your behavior had an impact on. In most cases this will be your victim(s) and your family members.**

Asking Forgiveness From My Victim(s)

Dear _____

_____

_____

_____

_____

_____

_____

Asking Forgiveness From My Family

Dear _____

_____

_____

_____

_____

_____

_____

_____

Second, you need to take responsibility for your **future actions**. Make sure you avoid the many irresponsible behaviors I outlined on pages 45-47. Indeed, no one wants to associate with individuals who avoid responsibility and blame others for their behavior. Again, you need to step up to the plate – no excuses for what you do in the future. Take responsibility by admitting your errors and improving upon them. Demonstrate that you are a person of good character who is willing to say *"I'm sorry," "forgive me," "can I help,"* and then move on to doing better.

Build Trust

Trust is the superglue of relationships. When you trust someone, you can **depend** upon them. You also like them – they are your friend. Violate a trust – lie, steal, cheat, scam, harm someone – and you may damage a relationship beyond repair. If you can't be trusted, what good is the relationship? It's simply an **abusive relationship**.

As an ex-offender, one of your most important tasks is to **build new and productive relationships**. And building relationships is all about **building trust**. If you can't be trusted, don't expect anyone to welcome you into their community. They want people who can be trusted – those who tell the truth, are responsible with things of value, and take initiative.

One of the most serious strikes you have against you is the lack of trust. After all, you already disappointed many people by violating the public trust as well as their trust. You need to constantly work at building trust among those who might otherwise avoid you because of your record.

To get started on this important journey to self-renewal, complete the following trust-building exercises:

1. Why should anyone trust you?

_____

_____

_____

_____

2. What have you done that would make people trust you more?

_____

_____

_____

_____

3. Among the people in your life, who trusts you the most? Why?

_____

_____

_____

_____

4. Who can give you a good character reference that stresses your trust-worthiness?

_____

_____

_____

_____

5. What actions can you take to make yourself more trustworthy?

_____

_____

_____

_____

_____

6. How should you respond if a prospective employer says *"I would like to offer you the job, but I'm not sure if I can trust you"*?

_____

_____

_____

_____

_____

_____

9

Seek Assistance for Lifelong Recovery

"Take the hand of those who can teach you to fish. For in the end,
it's the wise fishermen – not the dead fish – who bring in
bountiful catches each day to feed themselves and others.
Unfortunately, beggars don't know how to fish!"

MOST PEOPLE HATE TO ASK for assistance. They want to be independent and self-sufficient. After all, asking for help is often viewed as a sign of weakness and personal failure.

But there is a season for everything. And this is **your season** to meet the many people who offer a helping hand to ex-offenders. Some of them have gone through the same process you have encountered. Most share an abiding faith in the goodwill of their fellow man – they want to aid those in need of a helping hand. Many volunteer their most precious resource – time – to serve as mentors to ex-offenders.

You need to know about key organizations and individuals that can offer you helping hands. Most importantly, you need to know how to best relate to them. For in the end, your re-entry success will largely depend on the quality of the relationships you build. If those relationships are primarily with "old buddies" you used to hang out with before incarceration, especially the ones who helped get you where you are today, you may be looking at the hands of self-destruction. These may be the hands to hell!

One of the most important things you must do in the days, weeks, and months ahead is to **improve the quality of your relationships** – change your relationship environment. And then you want to return the favor some day soon – become a good friend and mentor to others who have traveled a similar and difficult path. They, too, need help in seeking redemption, restoration, and self-transformation in order to create their own purpose-driven life. And you can help others. Re-entry is literally a lifelong recovery process.

Learn to Fish With Great Fishermen

You've probably received lots of advice on what do to change your life – a combination of the good, bad, and not so sure. But this old and wise Chinese proverb is especially relevant to ex-offenders. It's my favorite success principle for everyone regardless of their backgrounds. It says a great deal about who you choose – your relationship environment – when seeking help in building new and productive relationships:

> *"Give a man a fish and you feed him for a day.*
> *Teach a man to fish and you feed him for a lifetime."*

Put this proverb on your wall, memorize it, and revisit it every day when you get up. It may inspire you to literally *"do the right thing"* as you go through the difficult process of recovery and re-entry. It should inspire you to seek out people who can teach you to be free.

Help should never be a just another handout or fish away. Rather, it should be a **hand up** and an important **learning experience**. It should result in building knowledge and skills for long-term re-entry success. You do this by seeking out those who can teach you to fish rather than those who will give you a temporary handout.

People who always look for free handouts develop a **dependency mentality** that harms their long-term

Seek out great fishermen rather than look for more dead fish!

recovery. Your goal should be to become increasingly independent, or free, by acquiring advice and assistance that will build a firm foundation for re-entry success. Therefore, seek out great fishermen from whom you can learn great things about long-term success rather than constantly gather more dead fish for short-term consumption!

Deal With Addiction, Recovery, and Relapse

Recovering alcoholics and substance abusers know all too well the importance of **redemption and self-transformation**. Perhaps you've already been down the road to recovery and have faced the great evil of relapse. Perhaps you've gone through the **recovery/relapse cycle** several times as you struggled with inner demons to make recovery a permanent part of your psychological makeup and daily behavior.

Or perhaps you really didn't struggle long since you are a person of heat, as I discussed on page 2. You convinced yourself that pleasure must precede pain, or perhaps believed that life was really not worth living for very long.

Each day millions of recovering alcoholics and substance abusers engage in a markedly successful exercise in self-motivation and behavior modification. They stay clean and avoid relapse by altering their **mindsets** and developing supportive **relationships** among fellow travelers who have been down a similar self-destructive road. In the process, they learn to deal with many important psychological issues – anger, self-esteem, love, forgiveness – that have contributed to their self-destructive behavior. They know the dangers of relapse, an ever-present evil that can put them back onto the disastrous and troubled road they have traveled for so long. Many learn to live a new purpose-driven life as outlined in Chapter 5.

Relapse is one of the most difficult issues anyone faces when trying to change their lives. If you've ever tried to lose weight, stop smoking, eliminate caffeine, control your libido, give up chocolate, or quit alcohol and drugs, you know how difficult it is to deal with your inner demons that contribute to your **addictive behaviors**. In fact, you may discover you have an **addictive personality** that also results in developing corrosive relationships that are difficult to eliminate. Indeed, if you've ever had bad relationships, you may recognize that your pattern of addiction is not just related to substance abuse – it also extends to **relationship abuses**. Since certain personal relationships can be even more destructive than drugs and alcohol, you may need to quit those relationships as soon as possible. Like substance abuse, recovery may be long and difficult, and relapse a looming possibility if you don't work the recovery plan.

Many people do overcome self-destructive behaviors relating to alcohol and drugs. Using AA (Alcoholics Anonymous) and NA (Narcotics Anonymous) approaches, they first admit they are substance abusers. That's very liberating! They acknowledge that they are on a difficult road to recovery, one they will be on the rest of their life. They also understand that relapse will be their constant enemy – always facing the temptation to fall back into bad habits and suffer the consequences accordingly. By taking personal responsibility for their choices and committing themselves to recovery with the support of other people, they develop an inner strength or **self-discipline** that leads them to recovery. They have clear goals, a support system, and important self-motivation skills to make it outside the bottle and needle. Recognizing the importance of self-improvement, they primarily associate with supportive fishermen who teach them that there can be a terrific life in the absence of self-destructive habits.

Get Community-Based Help

Who will help you with your re-entry, especially with finding a job? Will you be on your own or will you be working with various support groups? Who will you initially look to for assistance in your community?

Once you've been released, chances are you will return to your former community where you will seek employment along with food, housing, transportation, credit, health care, and other necessities of life. You will probably re-unite with many friends, relatives, and acquaintances, including former employers. If you are on parole or probation, the terms of your release may require that you become documented, live and work in one community, regularly see your P.O., disclose your criminal record to employers, and avoid certain jobs because of your background.

If you're lucky, you may be quickly hired by a former employer or land a job through a family connection or referral from a friend. In fact, these are the best sources for finding a job, regardless of your background – informal, word-of-mouth contacts that also screen you for employment and thus help you deal with the troubling issue of disclosure, i.e., disclosing your criminal history.

However, not everyone is fortunate to have great personal connections to quickly find a job. Many ex-offenders, who quickly exhaust their meager gate money, soon find themselves treading water as they enter into a scary survival mode – they need to get a lifeboat job **now** just to pay for basic food, housing, and transportation (see *The Ex-Offender's 30/30 Job Solution: How to Quickly Find a Lifeboat Job Close to Home*).

The first thing you need to do is to understand various **community safety nets** designed to assist ex-offenders in transition. A community is more than just a place in which you live, work, and raise a family. A community also is a place of opportunities to fulfill your dreams. It's made up of many individuals, groups, organizations, institutions, and neighborhoods that come together for achieving different goals. They provide **opportunity structures** for finding jobs through informal, word-of-mouth channels. They become important **networks** for locating job opportunities. Some of these networks serve as safety networks, but most should be viewed as **networks of opportunity**. It's where the good jobs are found in abundance.

The larger the community, the more safety nets and opportunity networks will be available to you. For example, the safety nets for ex-offenders in Chicago, Houston, New York City, Baltimore, and Washington, DC are much greater than in Sioux Falls, South Dakota or Grand Prairie, Texas. However, the opportunity networks may be fewer in large cities with numerous pockets of poverty and high unemployment rates than in smaller cities and suburbs that have booming economies with very low unemployment.

Meet Key Community Players for Ex-Offenders

Let's outline the key community players who can provide both safety nets and job opportunities for ex-offenders. They generally fall into these categories:

- **Government agencies and programs:** Social services, public health, courts, P.O.s, halfway houses, and One-Stop Career Centers.

- **Nonprofit and volunteer organizations:** Substance abuse centers, housing groups, public health groups, mental health organizations, legal services, and education and training organizations. Some of the most prominent such organizations that regularly work with ex-offenders include Goodwill Industries and the Salvation Army.

- **Churches and other faith-based organizations:** Includes a wide range of denominations that offer everything from evangelical to social services as well as faith-based organizations involved in federal government re-entry initiatives funding through the U.S. Department of Justice (see http://csgjusticecenter.org and nationalreentryresourcecenter.org) and the Second Chance Act.

A good way to look at communities is to visualize the safety nets and opportunity networks relating to you as found in the diagram on page 94.

Community Safety Nets and Opportunity Networks

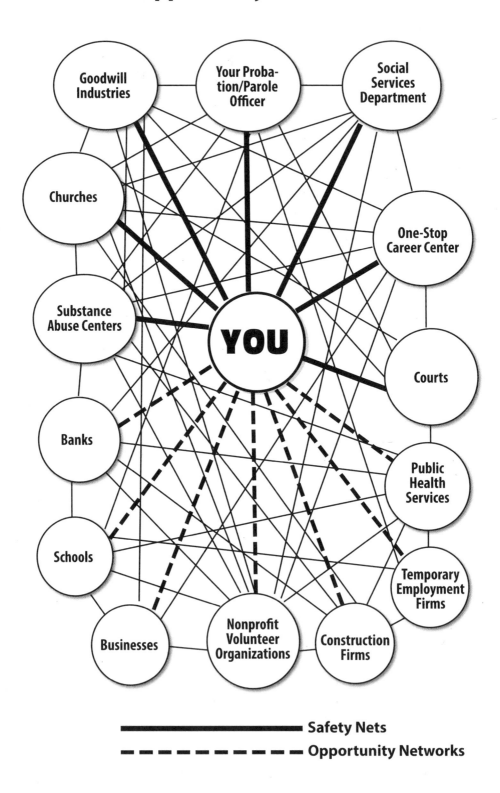

━━━━━━━━━━━━━━━━ **Safety Nets**
━ ━ ━ ━ ━ ━ ━ ━ **Opportunity Networks**

Let's take, for example, the city of Baltimore, Maryland. Each year nearly 10,000 ex-offenders are released into this city, which is anything but a hotbed of economic development and employment. Like ex-offenders in many other large cities, nearly 80 percent in Baltimore move into the worst neighborhoods. Recognizing that both the city and ex-offenders face a major challenge, Baltimore has been very aggressive in dealing with the recidivism problem and pulling together major community resources for dealing with the re-entry issue. In October 2002, the Mayor's Office of Employment Development facilitated the creation of the Baltimore Citywide Ex-offender Task Force to focus on ex-offender re-entry issues. The Task Force included more than 100 government agencies and community partners. In March 2004, the Task Force was succeeded by a Mayoral-appointed Ex-Offender Employment Steering Committee. The committee published a resource directory for ex-offenders, which outlined the major government and community-based organizations providing services to ex-offenders:

Ex-offender Resource Guide: Baltimore Community Services for Individuals With Criminal Backgrounds

This document can still be viewed online in PDF form:

https://marylandcure.webs.com/resource_guide.pdf

Many of these agencies and organizations function as **safety nets** and **opportunity networks** for individuals who are unemployed, homeless, hungry, sick, victims of domestic violence, mentally ill, HIV/AIDS positive, or drug and alcohol abusers. Examples of such service providers included:

Employment
- Baltimore Works One-Stop Career Center
- Career Development and Cooperative Education Center
- Caroline Center
- Damascus Career Center
- Goodwill Industries of the Chesapeake
- Maryland New Directions
- Prisoners Aid Association of Maryland, Inc.

Health
- First Call for Help
- Health Care for the Homeless
- Jai Medical Center
- Maryland Youth Crisis Hotline
- Rape Crisis Center
- Sisters Together and Reaching, Inc.

- The Men's Health Center
- Black Educational AIDS Project

Housing
- 20th Street Hope House
- AIDS Interfaith Residential Services
- At Jacob's Well
- Baltimore Rescue Mission
- Cottage Avenue Community Transitional Housing
- Helping Up Mission
- Light Street Housing
- Maryland Re-Entry Program
- Safe Haven
- Salvation Army
- SSI Outreach Project

Legal
- Homeless Persons Representation Project

- House of Ruth, Domestic Violence Legal Clinic
- Lawyer Referral & Information Service
- Legal Aid Bureau
- Office of the Public Defender
- University of Baltimore School of Law

Mental Health
- Baltimore Crisis Response Center
- Department of Social Services
- Family Help Line
- Gamblers Anonymous
- North Baltimore Center
- People Encouraging People
- Suicide Prevention Hotline

- You Are Never Alone

Substance Abuse
- Bright Hope House
- I Can't, We Can, Inc.
- Addict Referral and Counseling Center
- Crossroads Center
- Day Break Rehabilitation Program
- Friendship House
- SAFE House

Food and Clothing
- Salvation Army
- Bethel Outreach Center, Inc.
- Our Daily Bread
- Paul's Place

Baltimore also initiated a transitional jobs project, Project Bridge, for ex-offenders. It's a collaborative effort involving Goodwill Industries of the Chesapeake; Associated Catholic Charities; the Center for Fathers, Families, and Workforce Development; and the Second Chance Project. Targeted toward ex-offenders who are unlikely to find employment on their own, the project provides eligible ex-offenders returning to Baltimore with transitional employment, support services, and job placement, followed by 12 months of post-placement retention services.

Use Community Resources

Many large communities, especially New York City, Chicago, Detroit, Houston, Los Angeles, and Washington, DC, offer similar and different types of assistance programs for ex-offenders. If you or someone you know has Internet access, you can quickly locate such programs and services in your community. For an excellent summary of governmental agencies and community-based organizations assisting ex-offenders with employment, legal, and other re-entry issues, including referrals to other relevant organizations, be sure to visit the **National H.I.R.E. Network Clearinghouse**, which includes resources in all 50 states:

www.clearinghouse.lac.org

Other useful re-entry assistance websites include the following:

Government
- **Center for Employment Opportunities** (New York City)   www.CEOworks.org
- **CareerOneStop**   www.careeronestop.org/exoffender
- **Federal Bureau of Prisons**   www.bop.gov
- **National Institute of Justice**   www.nij.ojp.gov/topics/corrections/reentry

- **National Institute of Corrections**   www.nicic.gov/projects/
                                            offender-reentry-transition
- **National Reentry Resource Center**   www.nationalreentryresourcecenter.org
- **U.S. Parole Commission**   www.usdoj.gov/uspc
- **U.S. Office of Justice Programs**   www.ojp.usdoj.gov/reentry
- **Volunteers of America**   www.voa.org

Associations

- **American Correctional Association**   www.aca.org
- **American Jail Association**   www.aja.org

Nonprofit/Volunteer

- **The Safer Foundation**   www.saferfoundation.org
- **The Sentencing Project**   www.sentencingproject.org
- **Legal Action Center**   www.lac.org
- **Lionheart Foundation**   www.lionheart.org
- **Annie E. Casey Foundation**   www.aecf.org
- **The Fortune Society**   www.fortunesociety.org
- **Second Chance/STRIVE** (San Diego)   www.secondchanceprogram.org

Faith-Based

- **Prison Fellowship Ministries**   www.pfm.org
- **Re-entry Prison and Jail Ministry
  Resource Center**   www.reentry.org
- **Conquest Offender Reintegration
  Ministries** (Washington, DC)   www.prisonministry.net/CRM
- **Breakthrough Urban Ministries**   www.breakthrough.org
- **Exodus Transitional Community,
  Inc.** (New York)   www.etcny.org

Identify Your Community Resources

What is different among communities is the degree to which a community actually recognizes the need to focus on ex-offender re-entry issues. If you enter a community that
does not provide specific assistance and services to ex-offenders, you'll be on your own
in a sea of government agencies and community-based organizations that primarily provide employment and safety net services for disadvantaged groups, similar to the ones
identified for Baltimore. Therefore, one of your most important initial jobs will be to
understand how your particular community is structured in terms of such networks and
relationships. You want to put specific names to the various categories of organizations I
outlined in the figure on page 94. Once you understand your community, you should be
prepared to take advantage of the many services and opportunities available to someone
in your situation.

You can start identifying your community networks by completing the exercise on pages 98-99. Specify the actual names of up to five different government agencies and community-based organizations for each category that you need to know about and possibly use in the coming weeks and months. Remember the three types of organizations identified on page 93 – government, nonprofit/volunteer, and church/faith-based. If you don't have this information on your community, ask your P.O. for assistance, visit your local library and ask personnel at the information desk for assistance, do an Internet search, or contact your local government social services department.

Identify Your Community Safety Nets and Opportunity Networks

My target community: _____

Employment Groups

1. _____
2. _____
3. _____
4. _____
5. _____

Housing Groups

1. _____
2. _____
3. _____
4. _____
5. _____

Food and Clothing Groups

1. _____
2. _____
3. _____
4. _____
5. _____

Health Care Groups

1. _____
2. _____
3. _____
4. _____
5. _____

Mental Health Groups (if an issue)

1. _____
2. _____
3. _____
4. _____
5. _____

Substance Abuse Groups (if an issue)

1. _____
2. _____
3. _____
4. _____
5. _____

Legal Groups

1. _____
2. _____
3. _____
4. _____
5. _____

Other Groups

1. _____
2. _____
3. _____
4. _____
5. _____

The Importance of CareerOneStop for Ex-Offenders

One group you should become familiar with is your local CareerOneStop. Indeed, make sure you visit a CareerOneStop soon after release. It may well become one of your most important lifelines for landing your first job out.

Established under the Workforce Investment Act, CareerOneStops provide training referrals, career counseling, job listings, and related employment services. You can visit these centers in person or connect online to their databases. The CareerOneStop

System is coordinated by the U.S. Department of Labor's Employment and Training Administration (ETA). Go to their website where you will find special assistance for ex-offenders:

www.careeronestop/exoffender/index.aspx

This website is rich with all kinds of useful employment and re-entry information customized for ex-offenders.

Consider Using Temporary Employment Agencies

You also may want to contact various temporary employment agencies or staffing firms. This is good way to quickly get employed and acquire work experience. With temporary employment agencies, you work for the agency which, in turn, places you on temporary assignments with their clients. While these companies primarily recruit individuals for temporary or part-time positions, many of these firms also have temp-to-perm programs. With these programs, you may work two to three months with one employer who hopes to hire you fulltime once your contract expires with the temporary employment agency and you have met their performance expectations. Many large cities have over 200 such firms operating. Many of these agencies specialize in particular occupations, such as construction, accounting, information technology, law, and health services. Other agencies may recruit for all types of positions, including many low-skill, low-wage labor positions. Some of the most popular temporary employment agencies with a nationwide presence include:

- **Labor Finders**   www.laborfinders.com
- **Manpower**   www.manpower.com
- **Olsten**   www.olsten.com
- **Kelly Services**   www.kellyservices.com
- **Aerotek**   www.aerotek.com

Map Your Safety Nets and Opportunity Networks

Create a picture of the safety nets and opportunities networks in your community by completing the figure on page 102. This is a blank version of the example on page 94. Write down the names of the most important groups you identified on pages 98-99 as well as additional ones I've discussed on pages 98-99. Also, include the names of any individuals who could be key to finding a job.

Become More Proactive

Many ex-offenders have limited knowledge about the job market, unrealistic expectations about employers and how quickly they will find a full-time job, and a history of limited work experience. If you approach your re-entry with a positive attitude and realistic expectations – this transition will be difficult but not impossible – and take sensible actions, you should be successful. You must hit the ground running by taking actions that make a difference in your future. If you were used to spending lots of time sleeping, watching television, and exercising your body while incarcerated, it's time to spend more of your waking hours exercising your mind (read and do research) and becoming involved in activities that will advance your job search. As noted throughout this chapter, you can make things happen if you will:

- work with your P.O.
- acquaint yourself with groups and organizations that assist ex-offenders.
- approach your community as a network of opportunity structures.
- use resources that can quickly lead to job search success and a new
- record of work experience.
- avoid individuals, groups, and organizations that may waste your time.

When you get up in the morning, follow the advice of Brian Tracy in ***Eat That Frog***: first do those things you hate to do (eat the frog first) so that the rest of your day will be devoted to more enjoyable activities. Don't procrastinate by avoiding those things you hate to do. Clear the least enjoyable activities in the day by getting them over with immediately. There is much to be done in finding a job. Let's now turn to developing some realistic expectations as to how best to find a job.

Picture of Your Community Safety Nets and Opportunity Networks

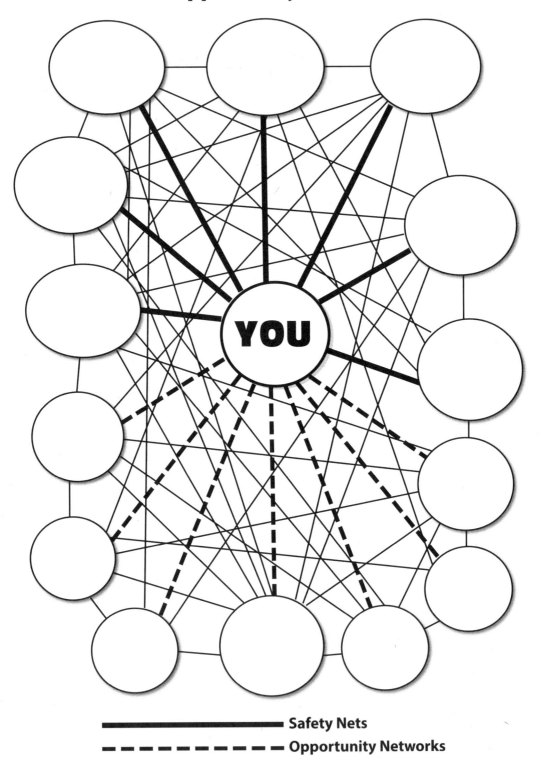

Safety Nets
Opportunity Networks

10

Leave a Legacy as a Good Friend, Spouse, Parent, and Citizen

"People we admire the most leave important legacies as friends, spouses, fathers, mothers, neighbors, and citizens. They have a positive impact on those who both admire and love them."

SO WHAT WILL BE YOUR LEGACY? This is not about what you want to be – your personal ambition or vocation. It's all about how you want to **serve others**. Are you going to leave this world a better place than when you entered it? This isn't about picking up litter, avoiding crime, or going green to save the environment. It's all about striving to have a positive impact on other people and society – make a real difference by truly touching the lives of others with acts of love and kindness. It's about stepping outside your skin for a moment and taking a hard look at where you are going with your life, and especially making sense of your "end game." You're not going to live forever. In fact, God forbid, you could die here today! Let's replace the selfish "me, me, me" with the **selfless** "me, you, and us."

Goals Are for Tomorrow, Legacies Are Forever

If you identified your purpose in Chapter 5, you should be able to connect your purpose to your lifelong legacy. When, for example, you wrote your obituary in Chapter 5 (see pages 58-59), did you specify your legacy? In other words, when you leave this good earth, what will you leave behind? Just more human trash and a fleeting observation that *"He finally managed to leave the bars behind when he was 27. Too bad he died at 29."*

What will your friends, family, and even strangers say about your life? Why was it so worth living? Did you teach a kid to read? Did you help a child develop important skills and learn lessons in life? Did you love your spouse as you swore you would – for better or for worse? Did you have parents who were proud of your accomplishments? Did you take your grandmother on a walk through the park and thank her for being a wonderful person? What positive impact did you have on your neighborhood, community, country, and the world? Or did no one really care that you existed, or even wished you ill?

While **goals** are something you set for tomorrow, next week, next month, or for a few years in the future, **legacies are final and forever**. They reflect your being and desire to serve – who you really are in relationship to the rest of the world. They give long-term meaning to what may seem to be daily struggles to survive. They are **not** about you.

What's Your Legacy?

Everyone should have a legacy in mind as they grow older and wiser. But it's especially important that young people begin thinking and planning their legacy. After all, you never know when your real time is up. If you believe, as many do, that we are all here on earth with a **purpose**, then this "legacy thing" makes a great deal of sense in helping us better organize and focus our lives.

> *It's time to begin replacing the selfish "me, me, me" with the selfless "me, you, and us."*

If, for example, you recognize that a lot of your problems relate to the fact that you came from a dysfunctional home where no one really cared nor invested time and effort in shaping your values, character, and future, you may want to make sure that never happens to your own kids. If you decide to become a loving parent and you recognize the importance of **parenting skills**, you'll work closely with your children to make sure they do well in school and life. You'll instill in them important **values and character** that will serve them well throughout their lives. You'll teach them the difference between right and wrong and the importance of developing healthy relations, taking responsibility, telling the truth, and developing self-control and self-discipline.

In other words, you'll literally become their **fisherman** (see page 91) who teaches them important life skills. You'll become a **role model** of a parent who insists your kids get a good education and do the right things in life. Indeed, you'll work closely with them in making sure they do well in school by acquiring strong academic skills, completing their homework, respecting their teachers, developing healthy relationships with other kids, associating with strong role models, and becoming active in school activities. Education will become their ticket to success, as it should have been with you (see Chapter 6).

Best of all, as your children grow up and become the persons you want them to be, you'll become a proud father or mother. You'll be respected by your children, who will most likely achieve success and may even take care of you when you grow old. And when you die, they will remember you as a terrific parent – someone who loved them and really sacrificed for them. That's love. You were a good father or mother, not a bad dad or mom. Despite your own background and struggles, you did everything possible to ensure their happiness and well being. And they will pass such values on to their own children, who, in turn, will leave this world a better place.

Learning to Love Others

Does that sound like a dream? No. It happens every day among parents who struggle to leave an important legacy behind – smart children who love and respect them. Not children of the **heat**, but children of the **light**, an important distinction we discussed on page 2. For these parents saw the light and shared it with their most precious possession – their children. They learned to love others rather than just themselves.

This can go on and on with examples of other types of legacies – serving as a mentor to someone in need, assisting the poor and downtrodden, taking care of aging parents, helping a neighbor get back on his feet, volunteering for community projects, or assisting someone with a physical or mental disability. In all of these cases, people become other-centered rather than self-centered. Indeed, their joy in life is to help others rather than to always help themselves. And that's loving others rather than just yourself. They give substance to H. Jackson Brown, Jr.'s other-directed philosophy on page 20: *"Remember that the happiest people are not those getting more, but those giving more."*

Meeting Legacy People

While your struggle to re-enter the Free World will take some time, along the way you will meet many wonderful and selfless people who will extend helping hands. These are **legacy people** – doing good because it's the right thing to do in their lives. They have a **calling**. Many have suffered their own personal struggles and tragedies. Disproportionately found in churches, temples, and mosques, legacy people also are found in many community-based nonprofit volunteer organizations and government agencies I discussed in Chapter 9 (especially see pages 93-99). Some of them have a foot in both the secular and religious worlds – they are committed making a difference in the lives of others regardless of religious beliefs or affiliations.

> *Legacy people do good because it's the right thing to do in their lives. It's their moral compass to serve others.*

Once you get back on your feet and have time to reflect on your experiences, do this regardless of your financial situation – feed the poor by volunteering just one hour a week in a local soup kitchen sponsored by a church or volunteer community organization. Or volunteer a few hours of your time on a local Habitant for Humanity project that builds houses for the poor – even though you may not have the most stable housing situation for yourself! Or help a disabled or elderly person enjoy some simple things in life, such as a walk through the park or consume an ice cream cone.

You may find such experiences to be transformational as you discover the power of doing good toward others in need. You'll touch lives like you have never touched before. And it will be good for you as you begin developing your own legacy force as an other-centered rather than self-centered individual. Never again will others see you as just another ex-offender – now you're a special person who loves life and those around him or her. If nothing else, your acts of kindness will be a form of **payback** to those folks who helped you get back on your feet and trusted you with their values. Such actions can become contagious and life-affirming.

Formulating Your Legacy Plan

1. **At what age do you expect to die?** _____

2. **Who loves you the most?** _____

3. **Who do you love the most?** _____

4. **When you leave this world, what do you want written on your tombstone?**

   _____

   _____

   _____

5. **What do you want your legacy to be in reference to your:**

   Parents?

   _____

   _____

   _____

   Grandmother and/or grandfather?

   _____

   _____

   _____

   Brothers and sisters?

   _____

   _____

   _____

   Spouse or significant other?

   _____

   _____

   _____

   Children?

   _____

   _____

   _____

   _____

Best friends?

_____

_____

_____

Neighbors?

_____

_____

_____

Church?

_____

_____

_____

Community?

_____

_____

_____

Country?

_____

_____

_____

6. **What changes do you see making in your life over the next five years in order to achieve those legacies?**

_____

_____

_____

_____

_____

_____

_____

_____

_____

7. **If you had all the time and money in the world to make a difference in the lives of others, what would you want to do with that time and money?**

_____

_____

_____

_____

_____

_____

8. **If someone gave you $10 million dollars with the stipulation that you could only spend $5 million on yourself, what would you do with the other $5 million?**

_____

_____

_____

_____

_____

_____

9. **If you knew you would suddenly die three years from today, what would you do with those three healthy years, starting with tomorrow?**

_____

_____

_____

_____

_____

_____

> *"Love is not just a feeling. It's a special behavior.*
> *Those who love are shaped by who and what they love."*

11

Action Planning for Re-Entry Success

*"Setting goals and planning are fine. But the devil is always in the details. For ex-offenders, that devil is called **implementation** – the fine art of translating plans into effective sustained action."*

N O AMOUNT OF WISHFUL THINKING will simplify the re-entry process. Re-entry is hard work and involves many psychological ups and downs attendant with unrealistic expectations, missed opportunities, and frequent disappointments. You often face the possibility of being rejected. And this is precisely the major barrier you will encounter to effective implementation, for many people are unwilling to take more than a few rejections. But you simply must take specific actions to effectively implement my advice in this book.

Making It Happen Despite Rejections

Planning is the easiest part of any task. In fact, many people get a "planning high" – they really love developing and re-reading their ostensibly cool plan. However, some people confuse their plan with actual reality. Indeed, turning plans into reality is one of the most difficult challenges you will face. It's relatively simple to set goals and outline a course of action without actually implementing those goals. But if you don't take action, you won't get expected results.

Once you take action, be prepared for rejections. Employers will tell you *"Thank you – we'll call you,"* but they never do. Other employers will tell you *"We have no positions available at this time for someone with your qualifications"* or *"You don't have the qualifications necessary for this position."* On the housing side, they may tell you *"Sorry, we're full"* or they may be brutally honest and discriminatory by telling you *"We don't rent to ex-offenders."* Whatever the story, you may face many disappointments on the road to success. That's okay. Such encounters are not worth getting upset about or fighting. Consider these to be "lessons learned" and move on with your life. This, too, shall pass, and you will be much wiser in the process of persisting to find your perfect place in the sun. Indeed, there are some wonderful tomorrows ahead. You just have to get through today and find them.

Don't assume you are rejected because of your background. While you may encounter them numerous times during re-entry, rejections are a normal part of finding employment and getting ahead in life for everyone. Rejections should be important learning experiences which help you better understand yourself, employers, and the job-finding process. More important, you must be rejected before you will be accepted. Expect, for example, 10 rejections or "no's" for every "maybe" or "yes" you receive. If you quit after five or eight rejections, you prematurely cut short your initiative. If you **persist** in collecting two to five more "no's," you will likely receive a "yes." Most people quit prematurely, because their egos are not prepared for more rejections, or they may believe they are victims of discrimination. Therefore, you should welcome rejections as necessary for getting to "yeses."

Get Motivated and Work Hard

Assuming you have a firm understanding of the seven steps to re-entry success, what do you do next? You must get **motivated** and **work hard**. Just how motivated are you to change your life? Most individuals need to be sufficiently motivated to make the first move and do it properly. If you go about your re-entry half-heartedly – you just want to "test the waters" to see what's out there – don't expect to be successful. You must be committed to achieving specific goals. Make the decision to properly develop and implement your re-entry plan and be prepared to work hard in achieving your goals.

Commit Yourself in Writing

One of the first things you should do is to commit yourself in writing to re-entry success. This is a very effective way to get both motivated and directed for action. As presented on page 111, make a contract with yourself in which you set target dates for achieving various re-entry milestones. Many of these milestones relate to a key activity for long-term re-entry success – finding and keeping a job that hopefully will turn into an exciting career. I address this issue in detail in *The Ex-Offender's Quick Job Hunting Guide* and *The Ex-Offender's New Job Finding and Survival Guide*.

In addition, you should complete weekly performance reports relating to your employment initiatives – the key to staying out for good. Focusing primarily on your job search, these reports identify what you actually accomplished rather than what your good intentions tell you to do. Make copies of the performance and planning report form on page 112 and use one each week to track your actual progress and to plan your activities for the next week.

If you fail to meet these written commitments, issue yourself a revised and updated contract. But if you do this three or more times, I strongly suggest you stop kidding yourself about your commitment and motivation. You need a better structure for implementation. Start over again, but this time find someone who can assist you – a trusted friend, a career professional, or a support group that will make sure you complete all tasks on time. Such individuals and groups can be the missing ingredient for keeping you focused and making sure you get the expected results that come with following each of the seven steps outlined in this book.

Re-Entry Success Contract

1. I'm committed to changing my life and staying out for good. Today's date is _____.

2. I will effectively manage my time so that I can successfully complete each step in the re-entry process. I will begin by spending at least two hours each day completing the seven re-entry steps outlined in Chapters 4 to 10.

3. I will make contacts with at least 10 key organizations (see pages 98-99) that can help me with various aspects of re-entry by this date: _____.

4. I will contact at least three people who might be willing to help me with re-entry by this date: _____.

5. I will begin acquiring all necessary re-entry documents on this date: _____.

6. I will complete my transportation plan by this date: _____.

7. I will secure transitional housing by this date: _____.

8. I will spend at least one week conducting research on different jobs, employers, and organizations. I will begin this research during the week of _____.

9. I will complete my job objective by _____.

10. I will complete my resume by _____.

12. I will put together my new job search/interview wardrobe by _____.

13. Each week I will make _____ new job contacts.

14. I understand the importance of rejections and how to best handle them.

15. My first job interview will take place during the week of _____.

16. I will begin my new job by _____.

17. I will make a habit of learning one new skill each year.

Signature: _____

Date: _____

Weekly Performance and Planning Report

1. The week of:_____.

2. This week I:

    - wrote_____job search letters.

    - sent_____resumes and_____letters to potential employers.

    - completed_____applications.

    - made_____job search telephone calls.

    - completed_____hours of job research.

    - set up_____appointments for informational interviews.

    - conducted_____informational interviews.

    - received_____invitations to a job interview.

    - followed up on_____contacts and_____referrals.

3. Next week I will:

    - write_____job search letters.

    - send_____resumes and_____letters to potential employers.

    - complete_____applications.

    - make_____job search telephone calls.

    - complete_____hours of job research.

    - set up_____appointments for informational interviews.

    - conduct_____informational interviews.

    - follow up on_____contacts and_____referrals.

4. Summary of progress this week in reference to my Re-Entry Success Con-
    tract commitments: _____

    _____

    _____

    _____

    _____

    _____

    _____

    _____

    _____

Planning and Implementing Your Weeks Ahead

It's important that you quickly get up and start running. Your first four weeks on the outside should focus on getting yourself established in a community. Your major concerns should be housing, transportation, clothing, and a job. Use the forms on pages 113-117 as starting points for developing your own large planning calendar. Start by setting major **goals** for the first four weeks and then identify specific daily **activities** that will contribute to achieving each weekly goal. Copy the form on this page for all weeks.

My major goal for Week #1 is to:

Monday activities: _____

_____

_____

Tuesday activities: _____

_____

_____

Wednesday activities: _____

_____

_____

Thursday activities: _____

_____

_____

Friday activities: _____

_____

_____

Saturday activities: _____

_____

_____

Sunday activities: _____

_____

_____

My major goal for Week #2 is to:

Monday activities: _____
_____
_____

Tuesday activities: _____
_____
_____

Wednesday activities: _____
_____
_____

Thursday activities: _____
_____
_____

Friday activities: _____
_____
_____

Saturday activities: _____
_____
_____

Sunday activities: _____
_____
_____

My major goal for Week #3 is to:

Monday activities: _____

_____

_____

Tuesday activities: _____

_____

_____

Wednesday activities: _____

_____

_____

Thursday activities: _____

_____

_____

Friday activities: _____

_____

_____

Saturday activities: _____

_____

_____

Sunday activities: _____

_____

_____

My major goal for Week #4 is to:

Monday activities: _____

_____

_____

Tuesday activities: _____

_____

_____

Wednesday activities: _____

_____

_____

Thursday activities: _____

_____

_____

Friday activities: _____

_____

_____

Saturday activities: _____

_____

_____

Sunday activities: _____

_____

_____

My major goal for Week #_____ is to:

Monday activities: _____
_____
_____

Tuesday activities: _____
_____
_____

Wednesday activities: _____
_____
_____

Thursday activities: _____
_____
_____

Friday activities: _____
_____
_____

Saturday activities: _____
_____
_____

Sunday activities: _____
_____
_____

Counseling/Assistance Organizations

If you need to attend AA or NA meetings or regularly see a counselor or other professional to deal with addiction and mental health issues, be sure to keep a record of your key contacts and appointments. Use the following form for recording this information.

Name: _____ Organization: _____

Address: _____

Phone: _____ Email: _____

Scheduled meeting time: _____

Name: _____ Organization: _____

Address: _____

Phone: _____ Email: _____

Scheduled meeting time: _____

Name: _____ Organization: _____

Address: _____

Phone: _____ Email: _____

Scheduled meeting time: _____

Appointment Calendar

Date	Time	Organization/Purpose

Parole/Probation Officer

If you are on parole or probation, make sure you know when and where you need to meet and always be on time and prepared for your meeting.

Name: _____ Organization: _____

Address: _____

Phone: _____ Email: _____

Scheduled meeting time: _____

Community-Based Organizations/Re-Entry Services

Be sure to keep a list of contact points (name, address, phone number) for several government and nonprofit organizations that usually provide assistance to ex-offenders:

- **Social Services Department**

  _____

  _____

- **Health Department**

  _____

  _____

- **Substance Abuse/Counseling Center**

  _____

  _____

- **Social Security Administration**

  _____

  _____

- **Vocational Rehabilitation Center**

  _____

  _____

- **Community College/Adult Education Center**

  _____

  _____

- **Library**

  _____

  _____

- **Church**

  _____

  _____

Documents You Need

Use the following checklist for identifying what documents you need to compile for starting your life on the outside. For example, you definitely need to secure a driver's license or state identification card in order to fill out a 1099 form with employers.

Documents	Source/Location/Action Needed
❑ Identification card	
❑ Social Security card	
❑ Birth certificate	
❑ Driver's licence	
❑ Medicaid card	
❑ Vehicle registration	
❑ Rap sheet	
❑ Military discharge papers	
❑ Will	
❑ Power of attorney	
❑ Insurance cards	
❑ Titles	
❑ Deeds	
❑ Court papers	
❑ Professional licenses	
❑ Professional certificates	
❑ Diplomas	

Important Hotline and Helpline Numbers

Many organizations maintain hotlines and helplines to assist the public with a variety of addiction and abuse issues. Some organizations now have mobile apps you can download onto your smart phone as well as Q&A and search sections on their websites. You may find several of these services useful:

- AIDS National Hotline   1-800-232-4636, cdcinfo@cdc.gov
- (SAMHSA's National Helpline)   samhsa.gov
- Alcoholics Anonymous   aa.org
- Be Sober Hotline   1-800-BE-SOBER
- Domestic Violence Hotline   1-800-799-7233, thehotline.org
- Drug/Alcohol Treatment Hotline 1-800-662-4357
- Gamblers Anonymous   1-800-GAMBLER, www.gamblersanonymous.org
- Narcotics Anonymous   1-800-992-0401, na.org
- Relapse Prevention Hotline   1-888-599-4340, www.recovery.org
- Suicide & Crisis Hotline   988

References

Be sure to compile information on at least three very selective references. These references could very well become your bridge to re-entry success. You'll need these references when applying for a job or doing any business that requires character and financial references.

When looking for a job, be sure to include references from individuals who know your work behavior, especially such soft skills or positive characteristics as coming to work on time, attention to detail, accuracy, dependability, character, honesty, and others I summarized on page 49.

Research among employers who hire ex-offenders stresses the important of **work references**. Employers much prefer such references over those that come from prison personnel or individuals associated with faith-based organizations. Employers see prison and faith-based references as weak, because such referrers are known to literally give ex-offenders a "pass" in hopes that they will succeed rather than accurate information on the ex-offender's real character and work performance. Employer references are especially prized because they relate to actual observable work behavior.

Whatever you do, select the best three references you can find. Ask each person if it would be okay if you used them as a reference. Also, send them a copy of your resume.

Name: _____ Organization: _____

Address: _____

Phone: _____ Email: _____

Type of reference: _____

Name: _____ Organization: _____

Address: _____

Phone: _____ Email: _____

Type of reference: _____

Name: _____ Organization: _____

Address: _____

Phone: _____ Email: _____

Type of reference: _____

Budgeting

The Free World can be a very expensive world. Indeed, one of your very first challenges will be to find housing – a major expense in most budgets. Many ex-offenders begin their new life in transitional housing and then fall through the cracks by moving on to the streets and periodically into homeless shelters.

You've got to do better than that if you're going to survive the re-entry process. Treat any transitional housing situation as the first step up in the process of finding permanent housing with a stable address. If you can't solve your housing problem, chances are you will have problems finding and keeping a job.

If you want to secure decent housing and meet other monthly living expenses, you'll need to find a job that pays above minimum wages. You'll need a full-time (40 hours a week) job that pays $15.00 to $20.00 per hour. If you're making under $12.00 an hour, you'll have difficulty renting an apartment and meeting other living expenses. Whatever you do, get your housing situation under immediate control so you can find a decent job that will provide you with financial stability and a stable base for advancing economically.

Examine the following budget items to estimate your ongoing monthly costs and then calculate what you'll need to make in order to meet those costs. Keep in mind that you should anticipate some major expenses when renting a room or apartment and arranging for utilities such as electricity and phone. Since you probably don't have a credit history, you may have to put down at least one month's rent and security deposits for activating your phone, water, electrical, and cable. You may also have the additional expense of furnishing an apartment – a cost that can be minimized by visiting the Salvation Army, Goodwill Industries, Habitat for Humanity, or other thrift stores.

Projected Monthly Expenses

Expense	Low	Medium	High
▪ Housing/rent			
▪ Household goods			
▪ Food/groceries			
▪ Transportation			
▪ Clothing			
▪ Phone			
▪ Electricity			
▪ Gas			
▪ Water			
▪ Insurance:			
- Auto			
- Health			
- Dental			
- Life			
▪ Interest payments			

- Cable TV _____ _____ _____
- Internet access _____ _____ _____
- Car payment _____ _____ _____
- Maintenance/repairs _____ _____ _____
- Fees _____ _____ _____
- Memberships _____ _____ _____
- Donations _____ _____ _____
- Entertainment _____ _____ _____
- Haircut _____ _____ _____
- Medical expenses:
  - Doctor _____ _____ _____
  - Medications _____ _____ _____
  - Dentist _____ _____ _____
  - Personal items _____ _____ _____
- Restitution _____ _____ _____
- Child support _____ _____ _____
- Child care _____ _____ _____
- Savings _____ _____ _____
- Other _____ _____ _____
- Other _____ _____ _____
- Other _____ _____ _____
- Other _____ _____ _____
  TOTALS _____ _____ _____

Projected Monthly Income

Income source	Low	Medium	High
Salary/wages	_____	_____	_____
Salary/wages of spouse	_____	_____	_____
Extra earnings	_____	_____	_____
Loans	_____	_____	_____
Other	_____	_____	_____
Other	_____	_____	_____
Other	_____	_____	_____
TOTALS	_____	_____	_____

Which is higher? Your monthly income or your monthly expenses? Use this projection information for planning the financial side of your re-entry plan. Does your plan include these cost-of-living and income elements? If not, be sure to incorporate them into your thinking for re-entry success. Pay particular attention to the close relationship between your big-ticket expense and income streams – housing and a job.

Your Essential Profile

Complete the following two-page form as thoroughly as possible. Once finished, it should serve as your record and quick reference in providing personal information required in applying for housing, employment, assistance, education, credit, and other resources.

Name: _____
                 First   *Middle*   *Last*

Address: _____
               Street   *City*   *State*   *Zip*

Phone: _____
               Home   *Mobile*

Email: _____

Birthdate: _____ **Place of Birth:** _____
        Month/Day/Year   *City/State/Country*

Social Security Number: _____

Marital Status: (circle one)   Single   Married   Divorced   Widow/Widower

Highest education level: _____

Schools attended beyond 8th grade, with dates: _____

_____

_____

_____

_____

Special licenses or certificates acquired, with dates: _____

_____

_____

_____

_____

Driver's license number: _____

Military status: Veteran   Honorable discharged   DD-214 form

Employment history: (employer name, location, position, dates)

_____

_____

_____

_____

_____

_____

_____

Special skills:

_____

_____

_____

Special qualities:

_____

_____

_____

Why someone should hire you: (your 30-second pitch)

_____

_____

_____

_____

_____

_____

12

Surviving and Prospering in the New Digital World

L IFE COMES FAST THESE DAYS. Maybe too fast for our own good. Most of this "fastness" relates to the role of digital communication in a world evolving with increased distractions, chaos, stress, and anxiety. Unless you are on top of this communication game, it's not a very ex-offender-friendly world for those re-entering after a few years of lockdown in mind-numbing correctional institutions surrounded by firewalls, scary people, anger, and hopelessness.

Back to the Future

If you've been locked up for several years, chances are your punishment included little or no Internet access nor experience with the latest communication technologies. Cut off from major modes of communication (email, texting, telephone) in the Free World, you've been divorced from the rapidly changing electronic world that has revolutionized the rest of society, including the latest in face and voice recognition and breakthroughs in artificial intelligence (AI). Maybe that's not all bad. Indeed, you lost the constant "connectivity" that characterizes and defines the sustained "busyness" of the increasingly unhealthy, stressed-out Free World. If you once were, you're probably no longer a stressed-out communication junkie! Your stress comes from elsewhere.

You're entering a new, chaotic, and highly competitive and predatory electronic world where you'll become an electronic "user" and a targeted consumer/client.

Not surprisingly, your caged communication has been somewhat primitive – a form of rehab. If you had limited Internet access (now available in prisons of only a few states), it was severely restricted. In fact, going to jail or prison may have resulted in technology withdrawal and illiteracy as you lost your computer, access to the Internet, and use of a tablet and smartphone. Your main windows to the Free World were monitored TV, expensive restricted landline phone calls, censored letters, and questionable rumors. To discourage your communication and independent thinking, you may have been prohibited from receiving books from the outside world!

When locked up, you definitely had no privacy nor did you need to worry about Internet viruses, identity theft, privacy policies, scams, robo calls, telemarketers, or other disruptive communication. All that is about to change as you enter a new, chaotic, and highly competitive and predatory electronic world where you'll become an electronic "user" and a targeted consumer/client who may experience all the positives and negatives of having Internet access. As you'll quickly discover, this is anything but a Free World. In addition to being costly, it's a sometimes stressful, annoying, disruptive, and angry world.

Missing Essential Life Skills – The Electronic Illiterate

Now, everything has changed, and you need to get onboard as soon as possible. Since using the Internet, tablets, and smartphones are increasingly **essential life skills**, you need to seriously work on becoming Internet and smartphone savvy. You should quickly learn how to best use email, text, send files, conduct online research, access key websites, use apps (applications), and join online communities.

> *You simply must get connected and incorporate the Internet into your new life of freedom.*

I assume you will, or soon will, have Internet access. If not, I hope you will quickly get "up and running" with a computer, tablet, and/or handheld device that connects to the Internet. You simply must get connected and incorporate the Internet into your new life of freedom. An exciting, although sometimes scary and predatory, online world awaits you. If used properly, the Internet will quickly become your best friend for maintaining your freedom.

Welcome to a Strange New World

Re-entry may feel very strange when everyone around you seems to be proficient in using the Internet, laptops, smartphones, tablets, and other personal and professional handheld technologies. For many people, their lifeline is their **handheld device** – usually a smartphone – that keeps them connected 24/7 to family, friends, employers, businesses, processes, and things that occupy their ever-expanding digital world through text, images, videos, and voice. In fact, you may quickly feel like a fossil when you get out from under the firewall that has "protected" you from the outside world.

From a technological perspective, you'll have a lot to learn in the coming months. Employers and others you interact with, including banks and utility companies, expect you to be literate in basic Internet and communication technologies. They will ask you to open an online accounts, complete with user ID and password, request your email address, assume you receive and send text messages, tell you to apply for jobs online, use particular apps, scan and attach documents, create PDF files, and send and receive documents and files over the Internet. Wow! You need to become very proficient in this new digital world.

If you don't have email and Internet access, you'll find this new paperless and digital world to be increasingly frustrating and difficult to navigate. And the people you interact with, including employers, may think you're from another planet, because you lack the knowledge and skills to fully function in today's society. Soon, no one will want to work with such an "electronic loser." This is what many ex-offenders refer to when they talk about entering a "scary world" on the outside. Prison did not really prepare them for this New World. They are essentially electronic illiterates in an increasingly digital world!

In many respects, being "free at last" may also give you a feeling that you're very lost in this New World. It has changed dramatically, and you haven't changed with it! It's time to play catch-up and learn how all of this new technology can be used to your advantage.

Get Connected and Acquire Online Skills

One of the first things you need to do is to get connected to the Internet and learn how to best use it for your purposes. In fact, depending on how quickly you learn, you might be up and running after an hour or two of basic instruction. If you don't have a computer, tablet, or handheld device with Internet access, start by visiting your local **library** for information and assistance. Many libraries assist individuals without computers and Internet access. Some provide classes for those who want to learn the basics of Internet use and email. If they don't, the personnel at the information desk usually give advice on where you can get such assistance.

> *If you don't have email and Internet access, you'll find this new paperless and digital world to be increasingly difficult to navigate... and frustrating*

Some local churches and other nonprofits may provide similar assistance with the Internet and communication devices. They also may offer **mentors** who can work with you one-on-one in developing computer and Internet skills. Local career centers and community colleges also may offer free or inexpensive courses on how to use computers and the Internet. Alternatively, search the Internet for "Internet for beginners" and you'll find references to online Internet assistance, including guides and tutorials.

If you're feeling Internet dumb or rusty, I strongly recommend that you make a top priority – from Day One – to get an email account along with Internet access and online skills. Use the most popular search engines – Google, Bing, Ask, Yahoo!, Dogpile, and Yippy – to search for several of these subjects:

- Internet 101: beginners guide
- Internet sites that make you smarter
- Mobile web: smart phones and tablets
- Search engines and how to use them
- Email basics
- Editors picks: best of the Internet
- How proper online research works

These searches will result in links to several online tutorials that focus on each subject. After a few minutes of exploring the resulting websites, you'll be wiser for having done such searches. If you need to learn **how to best use a cell phone**, visit this website:

www.wikihow.com/Use-a-Cell-Phone

The **WikiHow** website (www.wikihow.com) includes a great deal of other **how-to information** on everything from education and communications to personal care, relationships, and the work world. Also, check on the popular **HowStuffWorks** website:

www.howstuffworks.com

If you need **inspiration and intellectual stimulation**, visit the popular TED talks website:

www.TED.com

If you get hooked on TED Talks, you may want to visit UniversityWebinars with its many live webinars and archives of educational videos:

universitywebinars.org

If you want to take **free online courses** from some of the top universities and other sources, visit these informative websites:

www.coursera.org   ocw.mit.edu
www.edx.org   www.khanacademy.org
www.openculture.com/freeonlinecourses   ed.ted.com

You're also well advised to periodically visit the **YouTube** website – www.youtube.com – and search for any subject you need assistance with. The website is filled with useful video clips on just about everything. It's especially rich with "how-to" videos – repairing vehicles and appliances, using computers and handheld devices, packing and moving, speed reading, writing resumes, interviewing for a job, using email and the telephone, and much more.

Embrace "The Bright Web"

After a few days of embrace, you may discover that the "bright side" of the Internet (what I call "The Bright Web") is essential to dealing with many re-entry issues. Avoid the "dark side" of the Internet, or The Dark Web (porno, pedophilia, illegal drugs, scams, terrorism, racism, criminal behavior), which is very self-destructive and can lead you back into jail or prison. Indeed, much of The Dark Web is monitored by authorities who may quickly identify you as a "person of interest" who needs to be monitored and possibly arrested for criminal behavior. As you will soon discover, there is little privacy in today's new digital world of heavily monitored videos, telephone communication, and Internet use.

Whatever you do, make sure you arrange to have regular access to a computer and the Internet. Use it for learning and for staying out for good. You'll be glad you did. It will greatly enhance your community re-entry!

Index

Re-Entry Success Resources

THE FOLLOWING RE-ENTRY RESOURCES are available from Impact Publications. Full descriptions of each as well as downloadable catalogs and video clips can be found at www.impactpublications.com. Complete the following form or list the titles, include shipping (see formula at the end), enclose payment, and send your order to:

IMPACT PUBLICATIONS
7820 Sudley Road, Suite 100, Manassas, VA 20109-5211
1-800-361-1055 (orders only)
Tel. 703-361-7300 or Fax 703-335-9486 Email: query2@impactpublications.com
Quick & easy online ordering: www.impactpublications.com

Orders from individuals must be prepaid by check, money order, or major credit card. We accept telephone, fax, and email orders. Since prices may change, please verify online www.impactpublications.com before ordering.

Qty.	TITLES	Price	TOTAL
Featured Title			
_____	The Ex-Offender's Re-Entry Success Guide	$22.95	_____
Re-Entry Pocket Guides			
_____	The Anger Management Pocket Guide	$2.95	_____
_____	The Quick Job Finding Pocket Guide	4.95	_____
_____	Re-Entry Employment & Life Skills Pocket Guide	3.95	_____
_____	Re-Entry Personal Finance Pocket Guide	2.95	_____
_____	Re-Entry Start-Up Pocket Guide	2.95	_____
_____	Re-Imagining Life on the Outside Pocket Guide	3.95	_____
Re-Entry and Survival for Ex-Offenders			
_____	9 to 5 Beats Ten to Life	$20.00	_____
_____	99 Days and a Get Up	9.95	_____
_____	99 Days to Re-Entry Success Journal	4.95	_____
_____	Best Jobs for Ex-Offenders	11.95	_____
_____	Best Resumes and Letters for Ex-Offenders	29.95	_____
_____	Beyond Bars	14.95	_____
_____	Chicken Soup for the Prisoner's Soul	16.95	_____
_____	Dedicated Ex-Prisoner's Life and Success on the Outside	19.95	_____
_____	Ex-Offender's 30/30 Job Solution	11.95	_____
_____	Ex-Offender's Guide to a Responsible Life	15.95	_____
_____	Ex-Offender's Job Interview Guide	13.95	_____
_____	Ex-Offender's New Job Finding and Survival Guide	25.95	_____
_____	Ex-Offender's Quick Job Hunting Guide	13.95	_____
_____	Ex-Offender's Re-Entry Assistance Directory	29.95	_____
_____	Houses of Healing	15.00	_____
_____	How to Do Good After Prison	19.95	_____
_____	Job Interview Tips for Overcoming Red Flags	19.95	_____
_____	Jobs for Felons	7.95	_____
_____	Letters to an Incarcerated Brother	18.00	_____
_____	Life Beyond Loss (for Men)	20.00	_____
_____	Life Without a Crutch	7.95	_____
_____	Man, I Need a Job	7.95	_____

_____	A Map Through the Maze	11.95 _____
_____	No One is Unemployable	29.95 _____
_____	Picking Up the Pieces (for Women)	20.00 _____
_____	Serving Productive Time	17.95 _____

Attitude, Motivation, and Inspiration

_____	7 Habits of Highly Effective People	$18.99 _____
_____	100 Ways to Motivate Yourself	18.99 _____
_____	Awaken the Giant Within	20.00 _____
_____	Change Your Thinking, Change Your Life	22.00 _____
_____	The Element: How Finding Your Passion Changes Everything	18.00 _____
_____	Finding Your Own North Star	17.00 _____
_____	Free At Last: Daily Meditations By and For Ex-Offenders	16.95 _____
_____	Get Out of Your Own Way: Overcoming Self-Defeating Behavior	17.00 _____
_____	Goals!	21.95 _____
_____	Making Good Habits, Breaking Bad Habits	27.95 _____
_____	Making Hope Happen	17.00 _____
_____	The Power of Habit	18.00 _____
_____	The Power of Positive Thinking	16.99 _____

Anger Management

_____	Cage Your Rage Workbook	25.00 _____
_____	Forgiveness: How to Make Peace With Your Past	18.00 _____
_____	Managing Teen Anger and Violence	19.95 _____
_____	Violent No More	25.95 _____

Special Value Kits

_____	77 Re-Entry Success Books for Ex-Offenders	$1,296.00 _____
_____	Cage Your Anger, Rage, and Violence Kit	899.95 _____
_____	Discover What You're Best At Kit	389.95 _____
_____	Ex-Offender's Re-Entry Prep and Success Library	1,699.95 _____
_____	Ex-Offender Re-Entry Success Guides (See page 136)	72.95 _____
_____	Help Ex-Offenders Achieve Re-Entry Success	429.95 _____
_____	Job Finding With Social Media and Technology Kit	214.95 _____
_____	Learning From Successes and Failures Kit	1,039.95 _____
_____	Mindfulness for Refocusing Your Life Kit	292.95 _____
_____	New Attitudes, Goals, and Motivations Kit	412.95 _____
_____	Overcoming Self-Defeating Behaviors and Bouncing Back Kit	299.95 _____
_____	Reimagining Life: Discovering Your Meaning & Purpose in Life Kit	209.95 _____
_____	Start Your Own Business Kit	389.95 _____
_____	Substance Abuse, Addictive Behaviors, and Recovery Kit	1,134.95 _____

Survival and Re-Entry Curriculum Programs

_____	99 Days and a Get Up Training Program	$799.95 _____
_____	From the Inside Out Curriculum	425.00 _____
_____	Co-occurring Disorders Program (CDP)	1,015.00 _____
_____	Life Without a Crutch Training Program	995.00 _____
_____	New Directions for Ex-Offenders	1,029.00 _____

_____	New Road to Re-Entry Success Training Series	1,219.00	_____
_____	Now What? Project: A Map Through the Maze Prison Intake,	399.95	_____
_____	Orientation, and Adjustment Program for Inmates	399.95	_____
_____	New Directions for Ex-Offenders	1,029.00	_____
_____	Prison and Jail Survival Library	569.00	_____
_____	Ultimate Re-Entry Success Curriculum Starter Kit (See page 136)	2,569.00	_____

Re-Entry and Survival DVDs

_____	9 to 5 Beats Ten to Life	$95.00	_____
_____	Best Jobs for Ex-Offenders DVDs	995.00	_____
_____	From Prison to Home	169.95	_____
_____	From Parole to Payroll (3 DVDs)	299.85	_____
_____	From Prison to Paycheck (6 DVDs)	939.00	_____
_____	Life After Prison	99.95	_____
_____	New Ex-Offender Re-Entry DVDs (10)	1,259.00	_____
_____	Parole: Getting Out and Staying Out	69.95	_____
_____	Road to Re-Entry Video Series	651.95	_____
_____	Starting Fresh With a Troubled Background Series	299.95	_____
_____	Stop Recidivism, Now! (3 DVDs)	295.00	_____
_____	Why Bother? Finding the Will to Go On	119.95	_____

Life Skills/Personal Finance DVD/CD Programs

_____	Buying the Basics	$199.00	_____
_____	Life Skills for Independent Living CD Program	1,319.00	_____
_____	Managing Your Personal Finances Series	540.00	_____
_____	On Your Own: Independent Living Skills	99.95	_____

Addiction, Recovery, and Relapse Programs

_____	Addiction and Recovery Library	$3,795.00	_____
_____	Living in Balance	475.00	_____

Subtotal _____

TERMS: Individuals must prepay; approved accounts are billed net 30 days. All orders under $100.00 should be prepaid.

Shipping ($7 +9% of SUBTOTAL) _____

RUSH ORDERS: fax, call, or email for more information on any special shipping arrangements and charges.

TOTAL ORDER _____

Bill To:

Name_____ Title _____
Address _____
City _____ State/Zip _____
Phone ( )_____ (daytime)
Email _____

Ship To: (if different from "Bill To;" include street delivery address) :

Name_____ Title _____
Address _____
City _____ State/Zip _____
Phone ( )_____ (daytime)
Email _____

PAYMENT METHOD: ❑ **Purchase Order** #_____ *(attach or fax with this order form)*

❑ **Check** – Make payable to IMPACT PUBLICATIONS

❑ **Credit Card**: ❑ Visa ❑ MasterCard ❑ AMEX ❑ Discover

Card #														Expiration Date		
Signature						Name on Card (print)										

The Ultimate Re-Entry Success Curriculum Starter Kit

#7143 Custom-design your own unique re-entry training program with this bestselling set of three DVDs and 225 books. This special kit brings together the best of the best in ex-offender re-entry resources for creating your own powerful re-entry program. Can purchase separately. All new for 2016-2023! **SUPER SPECIAL: $2,569.00 for complete kit of 3 DVDs, 125 workbooks, 75 pocket guides, 25 journals, and 25 directories – a $747.45 savings!**

DVDs *(From Parole to Payroll Series - $299.85)*
- *Finding a Job*
- *Resumes and Job Applications*
- *The Job Interview*

Workbooks (128-144 pages each)
- *Best Jobs for Ex-Offenders* ($11.95)
- *The Ex-Offender's 30/30 Job Solution* ($11.95)
- *The Ex-Offender's Job Interview Guide* ($11.95)
- *The Ex-Offender's Quick Job Hunting Guide* ($11.95)
- *The Ex-Offender's Re-Entry Success Guide* ($22.95)

Pocket Guides (64 pages each)
- *The Anger Management Pocket Guide* ($2.95)
- *The Re-Entry Employment and Life Skills Pocket Guide* ($2.95)
- *The Re-Entry Personal Finance Pocket Guide* ($2.95)

Planning and Implementation Journal (64 pages)
- *The 99 Days to Re-Entry Success Journal: Your Weekly Planning and Implementation Tool for Staying Out for Good!* ($4.95)

Directory (138 pages)
- *The Ex-Offender's Guide to a Responsible Life* ($15.95)

BESTSELLER!

Ex-Offender Re-Entry Success Guides

#6847 Bestselling guides to the whole re-entry process. These five popular workbooks help ex-offenders effectively re-enter society and the workforce. Used by state correctional facilities as key re-entry training resources, each workbook emphasizes taking responsibility, changing attitudes, and making smart decisions. Jam-packed with revealing examples, interactive tests, and insightful exercises. Easy to read and incorporate into ongoing re-entry training programs. 128-144 pages each. 2016-2023. Can purchase separately at **$11.95 to $22.95.**

SPECIALS: Purchase all 5 re-entry guides *(Ex-Offender Re-Entry Guides)* **for $72.95; 10 sets (50) for $679.95; 25 sets (125) for $1,520.00; 50 sets (250) for $2,779.00; 100 sets (500) for $5,099.00; 500 sets (2,500) for $23,499.00; 1000 sets (5,000) for $43,999.00.**

- *Best Jobs for Ex-Offenders* ($11.95)
- *The Ex-Offender's 30/30 Job Solution* ($11.95)
- *The Ex-Offender's Job Interview Guide* ($13.95)
- *The Ex-Offender's Quick Job Hunting Guide* ($13.95)
- *The Ex-Offender's Re-Entry Success Guide* ($22.95)